ED

DOWN THROUGH THE YEARS

The Memoirs of Detroit City Council President Emeritus

ERMA HENDERSON

With Michael Kitchen

First published by AuthorHouse 04/08/04

ISBN: 1-4140-7179-5 (e-book)
ISBN: 1-4184-2290-8 (Paperback)
ISBN: 1-4184-2291-6 (Dust Jacket)

Library of Congress Control Number: 200409676

This book is printed on acid free paper.

Printed in the United States of America
Bloomington, IN

Dedication

This book is dedicated to the memory of my closest friend, Dottie Battle.

Acknowledgments

I would like to acknowledge Michael Kitchen for his work on this book. Over a four-year period, while he was attending law school, he took the time and effort to sit with me and take down my story, research the details, and put it all together into a readable form.

Erma

There are so many people who have been helpful throughout this process of putting together "Mother" Henderson's story. I'm going to apologize right now if I accidentally miss someone.

But first, I want to thank Mother Henderson for the opportunity to undertake this labor of love. I have learned so much about so many things over the four years we've worked together on this project.

I'd like to note that most of the photos within this work are from Mrs. Henderson's private collection. Some may have come from newspaper articles, some from photographers. We certainly thank those who have given them to Mrs. Henderson down through the years.

I'd like to acknowledge Marianne Williamson. Marianne's arrival at the Church of Today in Warren, Michigan, in March of 1998, was the catalyst for my opportunity to meet Mrs. Henderson. Marianne started a Racial Healing group that met once a week at the church, which I participated in. It was through this group that Mrs. Henderson sought volunteers to help her put together this book. I had some free time before I began law school, so I stepped forward to do what I could.

I'd like to acknowledge Patrica Reese. Ms. Reese was the original contact person who volunteered to help coordinate the tape recording of Mrs. Henderson's friends, for their input into her story. Ms. Reese is self-employed and runs "Things to Be Done" in Detroit, and we did a lot of work together in transcribing the audio tape recordings of Mrs. Henderson's friends.

I'd like to acknowledge all of the friends/family of Mrs. Henderson who helped by allowing me to record them and for their support throughout the process. They include Reverend Ortheia Barnes-Kennerly; Dr. Arthur Carter; Jackie Woodson; Edith Brewster; Margaret and Al Fishman; the "A" team of Irma Jaxson, Coco Shindi, Louis Pettiway, and Leno Jaxson; Betty Appleby; Mary Robinson; Patrya Smith; Anne Francine Smith; Deborah Carter; Dr. Mary Speed; and Effie Bazmore.

On the research and compilation side, I'd like to acknowledge Michael Descamps, my Aunt, Marlene Stawski, Tom Killian, Kwabena Shabu, and Millicent Kakowski and Wanda Holmes from Renaissance Unity (formerly known as Church of Today).

I'd like to acknowledge Linda Puryear and Larry Nader, who were providing me the opportunity to write for them prior to working on this project with Mrs. Henderson. The opportunity and their editing of my prior work helped build my confidence in undertaking this task.

I'd like to acknowledge the professors at the University of Detroit Mercy School of Law who, whether they knew it or not, at times did not get my full attention in class because of my work on this project. They have helped develop a critical eye of my own in writing and editing my work.

I'd like to acknowledge the attorneys at the City of Detroit Law Department's Labor and Employment Section, where I have been clerking since the summer of 2001. They, too, have helped develop my writing and editing skills that I have applied in this project.

I'd like to acknowledge Lorraine, who kept Mrs. Henderson nourished during the many evenings I came over to work on the book. If there is anyone more dedicated to Mrs. Henderson's daily well-being than Lorraine, I must have missed them in passing.

I'd finally like to acknowledge my wife, Denise, who tolerated my Friday night "dates" with Mrs. Henderson, to work on the book, and for her willingness to help whenever she could; my daughter, Lori, who pitched in and helped Mrs. Henderson with some of her activities; and my son, Colin, who can finish writing the book he claimed to be writing, "Erma Henderson Stole My Parents."

Mike

"DOWN THROUGH THE YEARS"

Down through the years, God's been good to me,
Down through the years, God's been good to me,
Down through the years, God's been good to me,
God's really been good to me

All of my life, God's been good to me,
All of my life, God's been good to me,
All of my life, God's been good to me,
God's really been good to me

All of my days, God's been good to me,
All of my days, God's been good to me,
All of my days, God's been good to me,
God's really been good to me.

Bishop David Ellis
Greater Grace Temple

TABLE OF CONTENTS

FOREWORD
by Diana Lewis

Mother Henderson - that's what I call her. And she is just that. She is mother, mentor, role model, teacher. The list of achievements that help define her life are undoubtedly impressive. She treads down roads often previously untraveled by any other African American, let alone an African American woman! But Erma is more than a pioneer in the black community. Erma lives a life that transcends race and gender. Erma Henderson is a remarkable human being.

I joined the WXYZ-TV news team on July 4, 1977. As co-anchor, I immediately began reporting stories about Erma. She was running for re-election to the Detroit City Council at the time. This would be her second term. Of course, in covering the race, I continued to learn the history and reputation of this lady who possessed so much drive, determination and political savvy. But this was only part of her story. I was new to Detroit, I was intrigued and I wanted to learn even more.

Erma Henderson had a story that was easy to research. In 1938, only 4 years after she graduated from high school, Erma had organized a sit-in to fight for equal rights in a Grand Rapids hotel. She fought for equal rights in Detroit in 1946. In 1969, she began the fight for a fair criminal justice system - one that didn't automatically discriminate based on race or social class. This woman I was reporting about had been making a difference for more than 35 years - and she wasn't slowing down. Of course, Erma Henderson won that second term for City Council. But not only did she win, she won more votes than anyone else did and became the first African-American President of the Council. I knew at that moment that I had arrived at Channel 7 just in time. This woman's story was too good to miss!

Since then, my relationship with Mother Henderson has evolved from a professional one to a personal one. Although retired from the City Council, she continues to stay involved in politics and community affairs and she continues to make news. But most importantly she continues to exemplify strength perseverance and drive. I find it so inspirational that even though Erma has lost her eyesight, her vision for the future is as clear as ever. At a time when slowing down and taking it easy would not only be excused, but expected, Erma is still out there, preaching growth, personal betterment and community improvement. She takes a stand and has a voice. And she teaches anyone who will listen. She teaches a "never say die" attitude. She teaches us to cooperate; we must help each other and work together to make a difference in this world. And she teaches us to care for each other and our environment. Her lessons continue and I for one cannot thank the teacher enough. I am blessed to have had the opportunity to know her, to be her student, her friend and call her Mother.

PROLOGUE
Grand Rapids, Michigan, 1938

In 1938, Lela Wilcox, Geneva McNeal, Onslow Parish, and I discussed the possibility of attending the Michigan Republican Convention, which was to be held at the Pantland Hotel in Grand Rapids. As members of the Young Republicans Club for the 1st District of Detroit, we thought it would be a good experience for us to attend. I was twenty-one years old, and it would be the first election in which I could vote.

So we mailed our registration forms for the convention, which included the women's luncheon, and a room at the hotel. We were in high spirits, excited to be attending the convention as delegates representing our district. However, the reception we received when we arrived did not exemplify the Lincoln philosophy upon which the Republican Party was supposed to be based.

We arrived in the early afternoon, and were impressed by the majesty of the hotel. The inside was equally impressive, ornately decorated and expansive. We approached the front desk of the hotel, to check into our rooms, before participating in the convention. The man at the front desk gave us a blank stare as we stood before him, requesting access to our rooms. He said that there were no rooms available for us.

We looked at each other, silently wondering how we'd handle this. Our paperwork was mailed on time. So we asked the man about this, and he was adamant. There were no rooms for us. I was the president of the women's division of the club, and decided that we would take action to break down this discrimination. Instead of leaving the hotel, which I'm sure the front desk clerk and the management of the hotel would have preferred, I explained to the clerk that we had reserved rooms, and that we'd wait for them.

We set our bags and ourselves down in the lobby. Every ten minutes or so, I would return to the front desk and asked if our rooms had become available. He maintained that there were no rooms for us. Then I would remind him that we'd wait until they were. This was the routine.

While time ticked away, I came up with an idea. Each of us had sung in church choirs during our youth. We were four well-trained, well-tuned voices waiting for our rooms in the lobby of the hotel. So I decided that we'd start singing. My favorite song of the day was "God Bless America" which Kate Smith had made popular.

The four of us broke out in song, "God Bless America" our continuous anthem. We sounded so good, people coming into the hotel thought that the convention organizers had hired us to be welcoming entertainment. Over and over, we'd sing the song, in different variations and styles. Our voices reverberated throughout the hotel lobby.

Attention was drawn to our melodious protest. On a balcony overlooking the lobby stood the wives of Fred T. Alger Murphy and Harry F. Kelly, two of the leaders of the Republican Party. They were on their way to lunch. Noticing the scene, they invited us to join them, as we waited for our accommodations. I respectfully declined their offer. They understood what was happening. In a kind gesture, Mrs. Murphy offered to fly us home and back. She was commuting to the convention by way of a two-engine plane, and she offered to take us home for the night, and then return to the convention the next day. Again, I respectfully declined her offer. The obstacle set before us had to be broken. Abraham Lincoln, the first president ever elected from this party, would not have tolerated this, and that was what we were here to represent. I also felt that challenging the Pantland Hotel was certainly less dangerous than riding in a two-engine plane. I was not comfortable with flying in those days.

So our quartet continued singing. We took a break to get something to eat, and when we returned, I approached the front desk clerk. Once more he stated that there was no room available for us. I returned to my group, and we commenced with another version of "God Bless America.".

As the afternoon progressed, you could see the embarrassment growing amongst the hotel's staff Soon, the convention would officially begin, and more people were arriving. When conventioneers or other people planning to stay the night at the hotel heard of our situation, support for us began to grow. The hotel had to try a different approach.

Their solution appeared well meaning, but it was covert in maintaining the prejudicial policy that rooms would not be available to people like us. An African American man approached us. He introduced himself as the hotel's head maitre d'. He invited us to go with him to his home for tea. By then, we had been waiting and singing for a few hours. We did not want to hurt his feelings, so we accepted his invitation, and followed him to his home.

It was a large, beautiful house. He gave us a grand tour, showing us the dining room with French doors that led into a garden. Upstairs were four spacious and handsomely decorated bedrooms. During this tour, he offered the bedrooms

3

to us for our stay during the convention. We were young, but not naive to believe that the maitre de of a hotel could make enough money in these times to own such a lavish home. It appeared to us to be a distant annex to the Pantland Hotel, arranged for its unexpected African American guests.

I explained to him that the reason we joined him was to avoid hurting his feelings. We appreciated his hospitality, and the offer of accommodations. However, we needed to prove a point, to stand up for our right as American men and women of the Republican Party, and to have access to the room that we had reserved in advance. The maitre d' smiled and was very supportive of our decision.

We drove back to the Pantland Hotel. Again, I approached the desk requesting our rooms. Again, I was denied. Again, our quartet belted out another rendition of "God Bless America."

By this time, the convention had begun, and we needed to register. We stopped singing in the lobby, and marched together into the convention hall, by way of an underground hallway. Resuming our melodious protest, our voices sang "God Bless America", which echoed in the massive arena, as if it were the scheduled entertainment for the registration process.

After registering, we returned to the lobby. The evening shift was now on duty, and the evening shift manager said that they would be able to locate a room for us. The problem was that there was only one room, with a single bed. This was to accommodate three women and a man. When I asked if they could get an extra cot in the room, they located one, and we accepted the accommodation.

The room was small, but the victory was huge.

Spirit will make a way for anyone who stands up for justice. No matter what obstacle one faces, it is important to maintain the vision of what you are seeking, and pursue it. It was blatant discrimination that blocked us from receiving the rooms we reserved through our registration. However, we knew they had room for us, and we would not let their prejudicial practice prevail.

Down through the years, more obstacles were to come.

CHAPTER ONE
My Childhood

Down through the years, God's been good to me.

It is an honor to be sharing this time with you, and I hope that when you finish reading this story, you will be open to the good within you and that your life has to offer. Spiritually, you and I are the same. It is only in our thinking that we are different.

In the pages to follow, I will be sharing with you many of the experiences of my life. I have been on this planet a long time, and the experiences I wish to share with you compose pieces of the vast picture that my life has been to this point. They demonstrate that by allowing God to work through me, it has given me the ability to help make positive changes in the world. You have the power to do great things with your life, too.

My story is also a call to young people - all young people - to reach higher than you ever imagined yourself to achieve. There are opportunities for today's youth who wish to awaken their hearts and minds and bring hope and happiness in the world. The world needs you. Please answer the call.

It all begins with you, though, and the development of your mind. The Bible tells us to "be still, and know that I am God." It is important to be very careful when you make a statement that begins, "I am." As you read my story, pay careful attention to who I declare myself to be, using I am. When I ran for Detroit City Council in 1972, opponents tried to tell me who I was and why I would not win. They said that I was poor, that I was African American, and that I was a woman. I replied to them that "I may be poor, and I am African American, and I am a woman, and I am going to win this election." So think carefully about who you say you are. Again, spiritually, you and I are alike. It is only in our thinking that we are different.

Take a nice deep breath, and settle in. The Spirit of God has kept me busy over the last eighty-plus years.

*****

I was born in 1917, just fifty-two years after the enactment of the Thirteenth Amendment to the Constitution, which ended the institution of slavery for African Americans. Over the course of human history, 52 years is just a blink of God's eye. The enactment that ended slavery did not change decades upon decades of prejudicial thought and action. There were many struggles that followed, some of which I was a part of. There will be more struggles ahead. Change takes time. It is important to remember that even though our technologically evolved nation has opened the way to many forms of leisure and entertainment, we must not become less vigilant. Instead, we must continue the process of opening America's, and also the world's, heart.

Down through the years, we, as a people, have referred to ourselves, and have been labeled a variety of names. For the purpose of our experience here together, I will only refer to us as African Americans. I feel this is important because it denotes where we came from and where we are going.

8

*****

Detroit, Michigan, has been my home since I was thirteen months old. My mother, Rose McQueen, and I were welcomed into the home of my uncle, Starling Thomas Jackson III (who I called Uncle Jack), on Detroit's east side, in a neighborhood known as Black Bottom. The neighborhood was located south of Gratiot, with Hastings Street being the main avenue running through the neighborhood. The neighborhood was home to the African Americans who moved into Detroit during the early years of Ford Motor Car Company's existence. Henry Ford offered the $5 a day wage in his factory, which brought many people into Detroit, including African Americans from the south. Black Bottom was abundant with the homes of wealthy individuals who had moved out and into more luxurious mansions. Large front porches were common. The houses were constructed to last generations. Their spaciousness allowed for more than one family to live within them, and some became rooming houses for the transient Southerner prospecting for gold on Henry Ford's automobile assembly line. Social workers, like my friend, Catherine Blackwell's mother, knew where the vacancies were. They would meet people at the bus station and direct the next wave of job hunters into the living spaces that had become vacant because an autoworker had earned enough to move on and purchase his own home.

Black Bottom was not just a residential area for Ford's newest employees. Three hundred and fifty African American-owned businesses prospered on MacDougal, St. Aubin, Joseph Campeau, and Chene Streets. The nation's only African American owned pawn shop was in Black Bottom. There were twenty-seven physicians, twenty-two lawyers, twenty-two barbershops, thirteen dentists, ten real estate dealers, eight grocers, six drug stores, and five funeral homes operating within the area. And the practitioners of these occupations lived in the neighborhood. The doctors and lawyers did not move or live in the wealthier sections of the city. The whole neighborhood thrived on its own.

Now, with a name like Black Bottom, one would think there were racial connotations in its origin. However, the early settlers of Detroit named the area Black Bottom due to the rich, dark soil upon which they used to farm.

I remember nothing of my father, though I would have liked to have known him. My mother had to leave him because he was from a wealthy family. I believe they were in the funeral business. The relationship with my mother was not appreciated by my father's parents, and, for whatever reason, he did not stand up to them. Therefore, my mother had to separate from him, which led her to her brother's home in Detroit. Her grandfather, Starling Thomas Jackson, joined us shortly afterward.

There were three generations of Starling Thomas Jacksons. Perhaps there were more, but my uncle, grandfather, and great-grandfather, were the only ones I knew. Except for my Uncle Jack, they were preachers and knew the Bible by heart. My great grandfather was in his 80's, and was blind, and he'd have my Aunt Maudie read the Bible to him every night. Aunt Maudie was my mom's younger sister, and sometimes she'd rather be doing something other than read to him. So she would skip a verse or two, in order to finish. But my great-grandfather would always catch her. He knew the Bible so well, he'd stop her, and have her re-read the section, because he knew that she skipped over something.

Our first home was on Short Monroe Street, next to Lieb Street, just behind Elmwood Cemetery. At that age, I had no idea what a cemetery was. But there were beautiful roses growing on the other side of the fence, and I wanted to see them more often than my family was willing to pick me up and show them to me. So I begged my Uncle Jack to build me a swing so that I could swing high above the fence to see those beautiful flowers. He did. I loved that swing because it allowed me to soar above the barrier preventing me from witnessing the beauty on the other side. It is amazing how such a memory is still within me, and yet, it is symbolic of how my life has been. I could have chosen to miss the beauty the roses offered, or I could overcome the obstacle to see them.

Uncle Jack was a very special person. He worked on the assembly line at the Ford Motor Car Company, and found time to see to my childhood happiness. Besides building me the swing, he also built me a playhouse on one side of the coal bin we had at the house. But he really never accepted the fact that I was a girl. He would make up names for me, like call me "Jack," or other boy's names. I don't ever remember him calling me Erma. He and Aunt Rosa Lee had no children of their own, and I think he was determined to make a boy out of me.

I remember one of the many times he took me for a ride on his bicycle. He had me ride on the handlebars in front of him, and as we rode, my legs dangled near the front wheel. Well, this one time, my leg got caught in the spokes while we were riding. It was a painful day for the both of us. My crying and screaming was not easy for him to listen to.

Sometimes, Uncle Jack would gather some of the kids in the neighborhood with me, and take us for a ride in his automobile. He owned a Ford Model T. It was painted black, as they all were, and had four doors. The glass of the windshield was thin, almost like plastic. The tires looked like oversize bicycle wheels. Uncle Jack could fit five of us kids in the back seat, and Aunt Maudie would ride in the front seat. Most of the time, he would drive us out to Dearborn to an open field, where airplanes would take off and land. We had a wonderful time, playing in the airfield. We were instructed to stay within a certain boundary, but we could still get close enough to where the force of an airplane taking off would knock us to the ground and raise our dresses over our heads.

Uncle Jack would also take me to baseball games on Sundays. It was a discriminatory event in those days. White people would go to Navin Field to watch the Detroit Tigers. African Americans were only allowed to attend baseball games at Mack Park, where the Detroit Stars of the Negro League played. It was a small ballpark, with bleachers, and no structure to shade us from the sun. But we were witness to all the beautiful African American ball players of the time. I remember seeing Satchel Paige pitch. The baseball games were such fun, and I would hold the hands of my Uncle Jack and my cousin, Charlie Cooper, swinging between them to and from the bleachers.

Charlie Cooper was a special man, too. Charlie was a skilled tradesman, a millwright, at Ford. He was also a finished tailor, like my grandfather and great grandfather. Charlie's work commanded top dollar. However, as both Charlie and Uncle Jack loved me and helped to take care of me, they battled personal demons that resulted from deep emotional trauma.

Uncle Jack and Charlie served the country when the United States was engaged in World War I. The military, at the time, provided only low duties to African Americans, like my uncle and cousin, which included the gathering of bodies along the war-torn countryside, and burying the corpses. The men would pull bodies from the trenches, sending the rats that gathered amongst them, scurrying away. Upon occasion, they would be given other minor duties, but for the most part, they were the men undertaking the clean up duties of the carnage that the war left behind.

Uncle Jack and Charlie suffered agony and emotional pain because of this duty. Alcohol became a medicine for numbing their pain. But they were courageous men, not only to have served, but to have returned and resumed as normal a life one could after an experience such as that.

*****

Now, of course, there were those times when I was a challenging child. My family had a vacant room in the house, and they provided it to me as a playroom. I had all my dolls lined up around this room. One Fourth of July, someone had given me some sparklers. I stood at the window of this room, showing the lit sparklers to my friends and neighbors Lola and Olivia Neal. The houses were close enough together that we could talk to each other. Anyway, they suddenly started screaming at me. Then I realized what I had done. The sparkler had caught the curtain on fire. I tried to put it out, but it was too much for me, so I screamed for help. Someone from my family opened the door, snatched me out of the room, and someone extinguished the fire. Oh, did I get branded that day! Spanked with peach-tree switches off the backyard tree. I never wanted to see another sparkler again.

Whether I was having fun, or getting spanked for being in trouble, I still love recalling my experiences growing up and living in Black Bottom. The historians and other citizens of today may look back upon that area and that time, and conclude that I came from a poor neighborhood. I never identified myself as being poor. I never felt that way as a child. We lived in this large house with my extended family. My mother worked at different jobs, like polishing the marble at the Fort Ponchetrain Hotel, and she did some private, in-home care of residents in the neighborhood who were sick. She then obtained a job at Michigan Mutual Liability Hospital. Though the times were tough, she always seemed to have a little money for us. I never felt that I was poor.

My wealth was not material. It was my family. They were my source of joy, and I think I may have been theirs. I was taught at an early age to recite poetry and dance. Saturday nights, my family would take me to the Copeland Theater, the only theater in downtown Detroit where African American entertainers like the Whitman Sisters, were allowed to perform. African American comedians also took to the stage, as well as an occasional minstrel show.

Spiritually, our family joined Friendship Baptist Church, under the leadership of Reverend J. H. Johnson, and it was there that my spiritual roots began to develop.

Then, Sunday afternoons were reserved for my performances. My family would gather around and I would sing and dance and share with them what I had done during the week. This was a lot of fun. I would introduce my new dolls, or the new friends I met from the neighborhood. By the time I got to be nine years old, I was dancing the Charleston, wearing dresses that swirled around and were made for dancing the Charleston. These performances were also for my Aunt Maudie and her boyfriends. I loved her and was always interested in her life. My mother and I used to worry about her, especially on the nights that she stayed out very late. But Aunt Maudie and her boyfriend at the time, would attend my weekly performances. One of them, I remember, was a heavy man from the West Indies, who rewarded me with candy after my performances. My favorite boyfriend of hers was Walter. He was a friend of the family through his sisters and relatives, when he started courting my aunt. All of us felt like one big family. I really liked Walter, and I wanted the best for my Aunt Maudie, so I hoped that they would get married. Of course, she didn't marry Walter. She couldn't do everything I wanted her to do.

I realized later in life that during the years spent living on Short Monroe Street, I had a wonderful family that surrounded me with love and joy and peace and happiness. On those Sunday afternoons, they let me know that I was important to them, connected to them. I think this is one of the things missing from today's family life. In general, families are in disarray and distracted, so much so that enough attention has not been made to the needs of the child. It is the family that helps children learn to relate and bond.

*****

I remember my first visit to school. Not so much the first day in class, but how much of an adventure it was for me to get to school in those days.

There was a streetcar that they used to call the Little Dinky. A rail ran in the street, and a wire above the streetcar would guide it along its path. To ride the streetcar, you had to wait for it to stop. The conductor would open the door for you, then you would drop your money in the fare box and find a seat.

The rail ended at Lieb Street. Because the streetcar could not just turn around on its track, the conductor would have to engage in a unique process. First, the conductor would pick up the fare box and move it to the other end of the car. Then, he would manipulate levers in such a way so that the car would operate in the other direction.

My mother wanted me to attend Barstow Elementary, which was located on Congress Street, certainly not walking distance from home. So one morning, my mother walked me to the Little Dinky, and told the conductor that I would be attending Barstow Elementary. She gave him thorough instructions on where I needed to go. Then we rode the streetcar eight blocks down Lafayette Street, to Orleans. She made it clear to me that this was where I was to get off.

At Orleans and Lafayette, we met a man named Mr. Taylor. She introduced him to me. She told me that he would be here every morning to walk me the two blocks to Congress Street. Then he would watch me as I walked two blocks to the school.

This was how I, at four years old, was to get to school. My mother rehearsed me a couple times, until it was time to do it solo.

My mother would walk me to the streetcar in the morning on Monroe Street. The conductor would be there, going through the process of making the car run in the opposite direction. He would then swing me on board. He was so delightful, and I was his buddy every morning.

At Lafayette and Orleans, the conductor made sure I got out. Mr. Taylor would be waiting for me. He would walk me down Orleans Street, to Congress, where he would point me towards the school. He would say, "You go ahead, and I'll watch you from here." It wasn't until years later that I realized that the man's name was not Mr. Taylor. Even though I called him that every day, he never corrected me. I never learned what his name was. But the man was a tailor by profession, who owned his own tailor business on Orleans Street. I just misunderstood when my mother was telling me who he was.

The intersection of Congress and Riopelle was wide and heavily trafficked. The police officer assigned to that particular intersection was a huge giant. He looked well over six feet tall. When he saw me coming down the street, he would come over to the corner. He'd take my hands and pick me up, swinging me to the middle of the street. Then he'd do it again, to swing me to the other side of the street. It was so much fun. Occasionally, before I'd let him take my hands and swing me, I'd say, "Let me go get a pickle first." I would run to the store that was on the corner and buy a big dill pickle. When I'd come out, he would mockingly point his finger at me and say, "You can't take that pickle to school." I'd tell him that I could, and that I'd put it in my locker.

Attending Barstow Elementary was special to me. Unfortunately, the school no longer exists. But it is fondly alive in my memory. The adventure of going to school was fun, but some very special people also influenced me. My best friend was Katherine Baird, who was from Grosse Pointe. We only had two classes together, one of them the auditorium class. My friendship with her introduced me to the experience of discrimination. Katherine was a white girl, and some of the African American children became furious at our friendship. They wondered how I dared to associate with her, and it created some friction. But she was a person I liked, and the fact that our skin was of a different color did not matter to me.

Mrs. Thompson was a teacher who had an influence on me. She was a portly lady who was in charge of the auditorium class. She directed all the plays and music in the school. I remember performing in one of her productions, a play of the children's story; Rumplestiltskin.

There was also an African American teacher, named Bonnie Osborn. She was just beautiful. Occasionally she would wear beige suits to school, which I just adored. Since then, I had loved and worn a lot of beige suits down through the years. I ended up meeting her again, around 50 years later, as I was running for Detroit City Council. She was a sister of mine in the Delta Sigma Theta sorority.

There were challenges during this period, as well. It was while I was at Barstow that my family broke up from the house on Monroe and Lieb. I was about eight or nine years old at the time. My mother and I moved further west, into a shared living space with an older couple. However, less than a week later, my mother moved us into a rooming house at 1815 Fort Street, at Orleans Street, with the Green family. Apparently, the man in the previous home was trying to molest me.

The Greens lived above the Monterussos, an Italian family, whose arguing voices we could hear upon occasion. Once, my mother asked Mr. Monterusso why he fought with his wife. He'd say, in a strong Italian accent, "Spaghetti no ready, we make a big fight!"

After school, my mother turned to Mr. and Mrs. Mosely to watch over me. I had some challenges with other school children that wanted to fight me. My hair was sandy red, and I had a birthmark on my neck that looked like collard greens, which provoked them. Also, my mother was given clothes from Mrs. Green that her mother had sent up from the south for her daughter, Gladys. The clothes were very pretty, and when I wore them to school, other kids fought me. They thought that because I was cleaner, dressed in nice clothes, and perhaps a little bit smarter, they tried to bring me down. This was becoming such a problem that my mom arranged for me to go to Mr. and Mrs. Mosely's house after school. They lived much closer to the school than we, and were like my second parents. They lived with their daughter and granddaughter. I don't know where the Mosely's got their money, but they always had a big, black Lincoln to drive, plenty of food to eat, and the extra time and space for me.

There was a huge razor strap on the back of the Mosely's kitchen door, and I was threatened with it at least once a day. Old Man Mosely was determined to toughen me up. He would stand there with the strap in his hand, ready to whip me if I ran home out of fear and trepidation. But if I stopped to fight with the boy or girl who was challenging me, then, when I got to their home, he would give me a pudding or other dessert. Here, I was taught not to run from a fight, but to stand up and fight to win.

This was the way it was in my neighborhood. People would look out for each other, and help each other. This was the 1920's, and these people had come from the south, just a generation or two from slavery, and they wanted to make life better for themselves and their children, and for our people as a whole.

The entire neighborhood was full of beautiful people. Next door to us, on one side, was an Arab family. The neighbor on the other side was the Barros family. They were Greek. Their son, Charlie Barros, was my first real love. My Greek boyfriend. We would walk to school together and he would always report back to my mother what he thought I should be careful of, which made him sort of like a big brother. Still, I adored him. Around the corner there were other families whose children I would visit and play with. I became close with so many families in the neighborhood. I remember one time, I was in one home where a loved one had died. They taught me how to sing the Syrian mourning song.

Across the street from us was a woman who was the minister for Ethel Waters. Ethel was a famous entertainer back then, and whenever she was in town, she consulted with the woman across the street. Sometimes, I'd run across the street to greet her, and sometimes I would just stand outside the house I lived in, and watched her arrive and depart.

I would see most of the neighbors almost every night, when the crab wagon would come down the street to sell crab cakes with lemons and ice. The children would shout, "Here comes the crab man!" much like they do today for the neighborhood ice cream truck. Before Gladys and I could go out and get a crab cake, we had to be clean. Our dogs would have to be clean, too. My dog was named Lady, and she was an Airedale. Gladys' dog was named Pretty Thing. The dogs belonged to the Greens, and somehow I was chosen to take care of Lady. She had far more hair than Pretty Thing, which made cleaning her a little more of a challenge. Once we were cleaned and the dogs were cleaned, Gladys and I would go out to the porch, then run to catch up to the crab man. The crab cakes were our big treat for the night.

Then, we'd keep a look out for the merry-go-round that would come down the street. It would stop in the middle of the block, and all of us children, black, white, yellow, brown, red, and all colors in between, would form a line to ride the merry-go-round. It would cost a nickel to ride, and the man who operated it would stay there until he collected every nickel we had, before moving on to the next block.

Also for entertainment, Mr. Green would take Gladys and I to Electric Park, which was a small amusement park across the shore from Belle Isle. The

Naval Academy stands there today. We would ride the rides, view all the exhibits, and always had a great time.

Then, on Saturday evenings, my mother and I would go to the show on St. Aubin. This was our night out, where just the two of us would spend time together. She worked so hard and often, that these moments of time together were special. Mother-daughter bonding moments. I remember once, on our way back from the show, a stray cat followed us. My mother said, "we can't let the cat follow us home." Still, I turned back, looked at the lonely animal, and beckoned it to follow. My mother threatened me with a spanking if I continued to encourage the cat. I started to cry because I wanted to keep the cat and give it a nice home. But mother sat me down and gave me a long story about how we lived in someone else's home, who owned a couple of dogs, and that a cat would not be welcome there. I didn't fully understand why we couldn't keep the cat, but I dried my tears and we went home.

Christmas time was also special. We lived in these large, beautiful homes, and decorated them as best as we could. I remember one Christmas when the Goodfellows, a Detroit charity organization that delivered toys to poor children, which is still active today, brought me an African American doll. Dolls with dark skin were rare in those days. I enjoyed it and loved it. As the surface paint chipped away over time, it revealed its white complexion.

With neighborhood friends, Electric Park, and crab cakes, I was at home within this international neighborhood community. In later years, I would meet people from this neighborhood who operated stalls at Eastern Market, and who remembered me as a child. Seeing these friends I had known as a little girl, up through my days on Detroit's City Council, was a great joy to me, and it enhanced my trips to Eastern Market.

Just as it had never occurred to me that I was poor, it never occurred to me to like or dislike someone based on their ethnicity. A person's ethnicity or culture or religion was not determinative of whether I would be a friend to them or not. To this day, I don't understand why, to other people, this matters. I believe it must be a taught response, because at our core, at our innocence, we recognize that we're all one. We're all alike, despite our physical and cultural differences.

This neighborhood experience of sharing lives is what we are missing today. We lived side by side with each other, and shared all those things that were not family secrets. We enjoyed playing with other children, and when they grew up and married and moved away, we rejoiced together in celebration. Together, we also mourned whenever there was a death. The neighborhood was something we loved and were reared in, and enjoyed. Neighborhoods today seem to lack that quality.

This diverse cultural environment which I experienced at such an early age, helped to shape who I am. Because of that environment, my life was greatly enhanced and broadened. Our world has a vast diversity of people and cultures. I have experienced true joy and learned a great deal from the many different cultures of that neighborhood, and from many other experiences in my life. The important thing to remember is to love people at the level you find them. You learn to enjoy being with them and learning from them. They learn from you. You share elements of their culture that are important to them, and it becomes a part of your understanding. Then, suddenly, you find that even though you may have a different color skin, a different nationality, and a different religious background, you are a member of their family, and they are a member of yours.

*****

One of the biggest influences on me, growing up, was the church. When we first arrived in Detroit, the family attended Macedonia Baptist Church. However,

Friendship Baptist Church, which was under the leadership of Reverend J. H. Johnson, was closer to our home, and our family became members there. At the age of ten, I was baptized at Friendship Baptist Church.

God has played such a dominant role in my life and I will expound more on my spiritual growth in the next chapter and throughout this book. God's role does not center around a specific "church," for I find God in all churches, synagogues, mosques, and temples - in all places devoted to worship, and even in all places not devoted to worship. My early neighborhood experience exposed me to many different denominations of religious practice, as well as many cultures. And something my mother taught me which I acknowledge still today is that God is here, there, and everywhere.

*****

When I was ten years old, I had to transfer schools. The completion of the construction of Duffield Elementary and the shifting of district boundaries, directed me to this new school. I remember hearing that Duffield was going to be the first platoon-style school in the city of Detroit. I really didn't know what that meant, but from what I understood, it meant something special.

Duffield had so many excellent teachers, and all of them were great to me. There were more African American teachers in the school, too.

While at Duffield, music became a great interest of mine. I had always enjoyed singing and dancing, but at Duffield, my auditorium and music teacher - Mrs. Gladys Roscoe Tyler - guaranteed that we went to Orchestra Hall every Thursday to listen to classical music and the works of the great composers. She also had old records that she would play that we would learn from.

The family my mother was working for at the time, gave her a Victrola and their classical records. Mrs. Green's friends would also give us classical records. This broadened my musical awareness. The Green's also had a piano, but I was not allowed to play it. It was a player piano, so as the roller spun making the piano play a tune, I would pretend to be playing it.

In school, I had to identify all the great works that I had heard at Orchestra Hall. The teacher would play a few bars of the piece, and I would identify it.

Duffield holds a special place in my heart. I remember, many years later while I was campaigning, I was invited to Duffield to speak at a teacher's gathering. It was the first time I had been there since I was a small child. The stage that seemed so immense upon which I, as a child, had to stand on to recite the things I had learned, was surprisingly smaller. As I stood before the teachers speaking to them about my vision for the city, they were not concerned with my recitation of composers and their works. It felt more like a living room conversation, than the nervous recitation of knowledge. Yet, it was upon that very stage that I had learned to speak before a group, and vocally carry myself. I think this is a very important skill. As important as it is for a person to have a vision of where he or she is going, and what they are doing, a person must be able to express him or herself clearly, and without fear.

*****

Upon graduating elementary school, my education continued at Miller Intermediate School, which is now a high school. I was eleven years old. This was a frustrating adjustment for me, because I became aware of and experienced the undercurrent of institutionalized discrimination.

I had a desire to be trained secretarial skills. But the teachers encouraged me and guided me to learn skills related to housekeeping, like cooking and sewing. During this period, seven out of every ten African American adults worked in domestic and personal service occupations. When I told them I wanted to be educated to be a secretary, they informed me that the skills they wanted me to learn would help me become hired and maintain a job. I explained to them that I could be hired as a secretary, if they would just train me in those skills. It was one of the few battles I lost, because I ended up having to take sewing and cooking.

I never grasped the skill of sewing. I remember trying to do a flat-felt seam that turned out so unlike a flat-felt seam that my mother had to finish the nightgown I was attempting to make. This didn't make her happy. So she took the nightgown to the school, and insisted that I would not be forced to make another garment. It was too expensive for her to buy the material, and for her to take the time to repair the damage I had done in my attempt.

However, in cooking class, I surprised the teachers. When I was ten years old, I was one of the best bakers in the neighborhood, due to instruction by Mr. and Mrs. Mosely. I had baked more cakes and pies than most of the grown folks I knew. And they were delicious. My aunt sent me to Kitty Head, a neighbor who taught me how to bake a seven-layer cake without letting it fall. I knew how to bake jelly roll cakes, lemon meringue pie, and rice pudding, and then I would sell them for a little pocket change. So, going into that cooking class, I had an advantage.

While at Miller, I was involved in dancing. Dancing has always been a favorite activity for me. One of the dances we had to learn for a play at Miller was the sailor's dance, which would be performed before an audience of our peers and parents. In order to perform, though, I had to have a pair of white pants. There wasn't enough money for my mother to go down to Kern's Department Store and buy a pair. So she asked a doctor at Michigan Mutual Liability Hospital, where she worked, if she could borrow a pair of pants from him. He was among the shortest men there, and he was happy to help. When she brought them home, I tried them on, and they were a mile too big on me. Because my mother had to return them to the doctor, she could not cut the pants. So she hemmed them up to the right length. This allowed me to participate in the performance.

Miller pushed me to excel. Mrs. Wagner, the music teacher and director of dance and drama, would form singing groups that she would then take around the city to perform. These groups would also be featured with the great Olly Farrish, an accomplished organist who played at the Broadway Strand Theater during silent movies. And not only was I pushed in dance and drama, but also in the arts. The arts were extremely important at Miller. Every Tuesday, my art teacher would take us to the Detroit Institute of Arts. There, we would study the paintings of the masters. These activities pushed me further than imagined, and at age eleven, I felt that I was going to grow up to be some kind of great celebrity or person.

My memories of Miller Intermediate School are special. I enjoyed learning and for the most part, the teachers were good to me. It was a life of innocence and play, even though I had experienced the institutional prejudice of placing children on a career path because of their race.

*****

After I had started at Miller, my mother moved us again, this time to Maple Street. We lived in George and Lula Cutler's home. As it happened, there was a girl next door who was my age, named Lela Wilcox. We developed a friendship that lasted long into my life.

On Wednesday nights, Mr. Cutler would take me to the Universal Negro Improvement Association meeting. Marcus Garvey founded the UNIA in 1917, and is still active today. The UNIA sought to inspire African American pride and love, encouraged self-reliance, reported news that was of interest to African Americans, administered to the needy, and sought to establish nationhood in Africa. I remember that each meeting was almost like a church service, with all the singing that we did. It was also here that I was taught that Africa was a continent, not a country, and the immensity that a continent was. These meetings were fun and inspiring to me.

During this period, as I was physically growing towards adulthood, my mental horizons were broadening. I was still a kid, and had my share of fun, but I, too, was experiencing joy in learning.

*****

At the time that I graduated from Miller Intermediate and was bound for high school, the City of Detroit changed the boundary lines for school districts. Those who were leaving Miller would go to Eastern High School on Mack Avenue and East Grand Boulevard. This was a cultural shock. Prior to our arrival, Eastern was populated by very very few African American children. And the majority of the white students were from financially well-to-do homes. Most of us, on the other hand, did not have the kind of money for transportation or lunches prepared by the school. Interesting times were ahead, and I definitely played a role.

On a mental and emotional level, I did not want to go to Eastern. Rather, I wanted to go to Cass Tech. Cass was a school located downtown, closer to the business district. Its focus was on business and commerce. I thought this would be good for my interest in becoming a nurse. Somehow, I talked my mother into it, and I broke away from my Miller friends destined to Eastern High School, and attended Cass Tech.

I took an advanced math course. It was a level of math that would prepare me for a career in nursing. It was difficult, and I had wondered what this complicated math had to do with nursing.

But Cass had also had an excellent music program, which also drew my attention. The school's theme song was the Blue Danube Waltz. And its band was very talented.

After lunch each day, I would go to the auditorium where the band practiced. Some of the members were my friends. I would sit up in the balcony and listen to the music the band was practicing, sometimes staying beyond my lunch hour, making me late for my math class.

But, I wasn't alone. Every day, standing at the edge of the balcony, this jolly old man would be leading the band, pretending to be the conductor. He was so cute there, leading the student musicians in his imagination. I tried to figure out who he was, but couldn't. So, I assumed he was a janitor.

One day, when I overstayed the lunch period, the man came over to me during a pause in the music. He said, "I see you here every day. What class are you in?" I told him. He then asked me my name and what I wanted to be after I graduated, and I told him of my goal of being a nurse. We continued the conversation for a while. As it ended, he said, "I'm glad to have had the opportunity to talk with you, Ms. McQueen. I want to wish you all the luck, and I look forward to hearing great things about you." I finally asked him his name. "Mr. Comfort," he said.

At this point, I gasped. "Mr. Comfort? Mr. Comfort? You mean the principal of the school, Mr. Comfort?" I was so embarrassed I didn't know what to do. After that, I didn't return to listen to the band, even though he didn't scold me for being in the auditorium instead of being in class.

*****

I attended Cass for only one year. I wasn't really gaining any different education there, and my mother took the advice of her supervisor, and transferred me back to Eastern High School.

I would walk to school, and in those days a girl wouldn't be caught dead walking to school with a boy. So we girls would fall in line as we passed each other's homes, and walk as a group. A group of boys would catch up, pass, and walk ahead of us, and they would keep their distance, so not to be walking with us. They didn't even talk to us.

Among that group of boys was Coleman Young. He was a year older than I, and as you'll see through this narrative, his life's path and mine crisscrossed many times.

Though our gender-segregated groups didn't socialize on the way to school, walking back home was a different experience. Together, we'd stop at Elmwood Cemetery, on the opposite side of the grounds from where I used to swing to see the roses. We would talk to each other and get the boys to climb the fence and pick lovely lilac bouquets for us in the spring.

But that was the way it was. We would walk to school, even in the winter, when it was cold and snowy. For six cents, I could have taken the streetcar, and every day, my mother gave me six cents to do so. But I would walk and save the streetcar fare, and also save some of my lunch money through the year, so that I could buy her Christmas or birthday presents.

It was during this time that I was awakening to the problems within my community. It is in the high school year, I feel, that students should be fostered to think for themselves. My involvement with church activities began the process, which I will talk about in the next chapter. At this time, however, I was involved in the Junior NAACP, which was an activity not affiliated with the school. We met every Sunday at the YWCA, guided by Gloster Current. Gloster Current was the Secretary Director of the NAACP, and led a locally famous orchestra. He helped us to understand how we were to act in school in response to problems as they surfaced. Alberta Wright and Lydia Ginyard were two of my friends who were involved. Alberta wasn't one to really get herself too involved, but she strongly encouraged me whenever I challenged something.

And challenged things, I did. For example, I discovered an issue regarding the composite school portrait. The portrait featured every person in the class. However, the African American children were always placed at the bottom of the composite portrait. I learned that the reason for this was so that the parents of the white students could then cut off the bottom row or rows of the portrait, to eliminate the African American students, and display an all-white class.

I felt that this was wrong, and that it had to be brought to the attention of the principal. At first, I wasn't quite sure how I was going to approach him, but God provided the answer and showed me just how to proceed.

In my English class, the teacher assigned us to sit in alphabetical order, to avoid prejudice within her classroom. This placed me between two boys - Red Nichols and Joe Rubino. Red, as you can imagine, had red hair, with a cherry face that always looked happy, and big, broad shoulders. Joe had dark black hair, with tan skin and was of stocky build. I had become buddies with them, and we had made a unique trio - Irish, Italian, and me.

One day, I discussed my concern about the prejudice created by the composite portrait to them. They were good guys, and because this disturbed me, they became disturbed by it, too. I then realized I had a way to bring the problem to the attention of the principal. Joe Rubino and Red Nichols were the star football players of the school. They weren't treated any more special than anyone else, however, their popularity would certainly draw the attention of the principal's ear.

So the three of us scheduled an appointment to see the principal. I'm sure he was quite curious to hear what his two football stars and I had to say. Together, the three of us sat down with him in his office. I explained to him the problem, and Joe and Red supported me. At the end of our meeting, the principal said that he would give the matter some serious thought.

When the class portrait was released that year, the African American children were not in the bottom rows. They were dispersed throughout the portrait because the school requested the students' images to be arranged in alphabetical order. We had won our first victory. This had really united us as a team. Our unlikely trio would stroll up and down the halls, gathering information, studying classrooms, trying to uncover any discrimination.

One issue that arose was based on the speakers that were brought in for the general assemblies. Every student in the school would attend these assemblies, and I had noticed that there had yet to be a representative of the African American community to speak at one. The students benefited from having guest speakers come to the school, but without a balance that reflected the school's population, we weren't learning from or about each other.

That observation was all it took. Joe, Red, and I were once again, up to the challenge. By this time, the principal had become quite familiar with us. After another polite, but firm discussion, the principal agreed to get a representative from the African American community to speak at the next general assembly.

That day arrived. I met up with Joe and Red, and we were running a little late to the auditorium. When we got there, the auditorium was almost full. There were a few spaces open in the front, being held for us. As we strolled down the aisle, I could sense Joe and Red getting upset. They didn't see anyone resembling an African American speaker. They felt betrayed by the principal.

I grabbed each of their hands, as they were on both sides of me. "Listen, fellas," I said. "Calm down. Let's sit down and talk about this." They grumbled under their breath as we took our seats.

I recognized someone in the front row, and knew it would be okay. I pointed him out to Joe and Red. "See that man, there," I said, "The pudgy man? That's the speaker."

"He ain't African American," one of them said.

"Now wait a minute. That's Reverend Robert L. Bradby. He's the pastor of Second Baptist Church, the oldest church in the African American community. That church has a part of the underground railroad beneath it." The boys were beginning to calm down. "The principal didn't lie to us," I said. "The speaker is from the African American community. He just happens to be a light-complected African American." The Reverend spoke, and we all benefited by what he had to say.

This was the way high school was for me. With the help of my friends, we'd uncover problems and create solutions. I wish kids today would focus more on recognizing things around them that are inherently wrong, and work towards solving them. With situations like the incident at Columbine High School, teenage depression, eating disorders, drug and alcohol use, pregnancy, self-mutilation, and suicide, there are plenty of problems that create these results. Instead, video games, the Internet, and television pre-occupy their minds, blinding them from the solutions. Without a vision, the people perish.

*****

There are people today who have called me the Mother of Detroit. That is quite an honor to me. As I look back, down through the years, so many children, of so many ages, I have adopted as family, and they have adopted me. This sense of being a mother for Detroit citizens, caring for Detroit citizens, and others from all around the world, stretched back to my childhood years, and it started with my first Godchild.

Agatha Freeman was a friend of mine at Eastern High School. She came from a large family, she being one of seven children. Her father owned City Cab Company, one of the first African American cab companies, which helped him provide for such a large family. And her mother was one of the nicest women you'd ever meet.

Agatha's mother was pregnant again. And one evening, I heard that Mr. Freeman had taken her to the hospital, to have the baby. She couldn't go to Harper Hospital, because at that time they would not accept African American patients.

Rather, across the street in a large house, was a hospital for African American patients. When I arrived, the scene was something you wouldn't imagine at a hospital. The room was wall-to-wall beds, with patients on them. I found Mr. Freeman, who pointed me towards Mrs. Freeman. She rested, looking weak and tired. I asked her if she had been properly cleaned (here I was, this Junior Nurse from Calvary Baptist thinking she might know a thing or two about nursing). Mrs. Freeman said no. I asked her when they were going to take the baby, and she said that the baby had already come, and they had taken it away from her.

So I went to find out where the baby was, and when I found her, I was appalled. The baby, so tiny, no bigger than your hand, was laying naked and exposed, without any blankets. Mr. Freeman heard my shouting for a nurse or doctor, and came to see what the commotion was. One of the nurses said that the baby was premature. It was born six months into Mrs. Freeman's pregnancy. I found something to wrap the baby in, and gave the baby to Mr. Freeman. "Take this baby to Harper Hospital, across the street," I told him. He was reluctant because Harper Hospital did not accept African Americans. So together, we went across the street with the baby, and the physicians took one look at the baby, and jumped into action. They didn't care that we were African American at that point. Their natural desire to help and heal took over.

The baby stayed in the hospital for six months, under their watchful care. They said that no premature baby, born three months early, had ever survived at their hospital, until this one.

When the baby was released from the hospital, Mrs. Freeman had already died. Because she had had eight children, and had not been properly cared for, she did not survive this, her last, pregnancy. But I felt somewhat responsible for the baby, having taken her to Harper Hospital and getting her the care she needed. I'd visit her often, in the hospital, and after she was released.

Mr. Freeman invited me to attend the baby's christening. He told me that he wanted me to be her Godmother, and to name the baby. I was honored. I named her Phyllis, after my grandmother. Mr. Freeman and I stood before the reverend at Calvary Baptist Church, with little Phyllis, the first of my many Godchildren to come.

Mr. Freeman re-married, and moved out into the country with his new wife, and the eight children. I didn't see much of Phyllis, but did keep up with what she was doing. Her step-mom got her interested in music, which I appreciated.

In the 1980's, while I was on City Council, Phyllis took ill. The German Chancellor had invited myself and other city council members from around the nation, to visit Germany. All the plans were made, and it was on the eve of my leaving that I received news about Phyllis. I went to the hospital, and said my good bye. She was not well at all, not expected to live through the week. She died a day or two later.

*****

Because of our move to Maple Street, back when I started school at Miller Intermediate, my mother began taking us to Calvary Baptist Church. I was very involved at Calvary, which I will speak to later in the narrative. However, one of my activities at Calvary led me to a glorious moment in my high school days.

At Calvary, I was in the junior choir. There were a few of us who attended Eastern High School and sang in Calvary's junior choir. However, Mrs. Grace, the school's glee club director, chose the singers for the glee club very selectively, not allowing some students the opportunity to audition. So, there were four of us; Ruth Jean Hutchins, Sadie Young, Roberta Smith, and myself, who sang in the junior choir every Sunday at Calvary. We felt that we deserved to at least be heard, before Mrs. Grace could determine that we could not sing. Another girl, Reatha McCallums, joined us, and together, we approached Mrs. Grace, insisting to be heard. After some hesitation, she finally agreed. Once she heard us, she accepted all of us into the girl's glee club. Roberta and I were sopranos, Sadie was a contralto, and Ruth Jean an alto.

Towards the end of the school year, Harold Love approached Mrs. Grace and the girl's glee club. Mr. Love led the boy's glee club, which was famous throughout Michigan because he took them to perform at churches, halls, and prisons around the state. His interest in the girl's glee club was because he was going to have the boy's glee club perform "Lieberstrum" by Liszt at graduation, and he needed a soprano whose voice would compliment the violins. He auditioned each of the girls, and when he was finished he pointed at me. "I want this one, Erma McQueen." Well, I almost fainted. I was so honored to be chosen.

I couldn't wait to tell my mother, and when she got home from work, I gave her the news. She was so proud of me. But then, it occurred to us. For a graduation concert, I would need something special to wear. There wasn't anything in my modest wardrobe that would be appropriate. My mother told me not to worry about that. She dug into her cookie jar and gave me all the money she had saved. It wasn't much, but it would buy me a decent dress at Kern's Department Store. The basement of Kern's, that is. The upper floors had clothing that went well beyond my budget. And I didn't need to consider Hudson's, because even in the basement, the dresses cost more than I had.

I walked to Kern's with the money mother gave me. I didn't take the street car, because every penny was needed to put towards the dress. Upon arrival, I went directly to the basement and began my search. After browsing the racks for a period of time, a store clerk approached me and asked if she could help. I had found a very nice dress, however it was a little more than my budget would allow. I told her that I was looking for a very special dress, something like what I had picked out, but less expensive. She asked me about the occasion that I would be wearing it for, and I explained to her about my being selected to be the soloist at graduation. She looked at me and asked me to sing something. I thought that was an odd request, but I sang one of our school songs. She told me that she thought I was very good, and should wear the dress I had picked out. I reminded her that I didn't have enough money for it. She smiled and said she'd take care of it.

The woman took the dress and led me around the store, to the other clerks on the floor. She explained the situation to each of them, and each one of them responded with a small contribution towards my dress. By the time she was done, the clerk had collected the difference between the money in my pocket and the cost of the dress. I sang and danced all the way home.

This especially impressed me about Kern's Department Store and those clerks in particular. When I was sixteen, I had babysat Mrs. Ketz's little girl, Shirley. Mrs. Ketz was employed at Kern's. An African American holding a position in a department store like Kern's was unheard of. Generally, only the fairest-skinned African Americans would be hired in the department stores, and then, only as maids or elevator operators. But this was a part of Kern's. The overall friendliness and concern for people, demonstrated by their clerks, created a fond attachment in me towards Kern's. The building was distinctive, with a huge clock on it. Back then, it was a landmark, similar to Hudson's, and, as time passed, it was heartbreaking to see Kern's tore down.

A great deal of practice was required to prepare for the performance. Mrs. Essie T. Shaw, an accomplished pianist in the city who also played the organ at Calvary, helped me rehearse in her big studio on Macoma Street. Mrs. A. W. Hutchins, the music and choir director at Calvary, also helped me.

The night of the graduation was one of the proudest moments of my life. There I was, Erma McQueen, singing solo at Eastern High School's graduation. I was well rehearsed and well dressed. Had Roberta, Sadie, Ruth Jean and I chose not to confront Mrs. Grace, the opportunity for any of us to sing this solo would have been denied.

Eastern High School provided me with the opportunity to expand my potential, even though in most cases, it had to do with overcoming obstacles and making changes within the institution, rather than from the knowledge gained in the classroom. Even in the classroom, I was challenged to go beyond the material presented, and educate myself, my class mates and my favorite teacher, Mrs. Mae Graham.

Mae Graham was my history teacher and she was open to the educational process. I was growing frustrated in her class because the book from which she taught was full of antiquated facts. She would teach us something that would be a disgrace or lie about African Americans. I vented my frustration to my mother and she told me to go to the library and find the facts I needed to show the truth. So I followed my mother's advice, and every time that Mrs. Graham taught us something I felt was inaccurate, I would meet my mother at the library after school, and locate the true story.

For example, one day, Mrs. Graham directed our attention to a page in the text book that depicted African Americans in the legislature of the South as buffoons and fools. After school, I went to the library and returned to class the next day with a book with photographs of distinguished African American legislators of the South.

Mrs. Graham would allow me to do this, and teach the class whatever I discovered to refute her text book's story. I had become the teacher of my history class.

At the end of the year, I gave Mrs. Graham my yearbook to sign. I'll never forget what she wrote.

"Erma. Thank you for being my history teacher. Mae Graham."

CHAPTER TWO
Spirituality - From Roots to Never-Ending Connection

I Am a Child of God
Nothing can hurt me,
Make me sick, or afraid.
I am Spirit, Spirit is God
God cannot be hurt, sick or afraid
I manifest my Real Self now.

God is my life. This I must make clear, because without my connection to God, I would not have been able to achieve so much in my life. Without my connection to God, my memoirs would not be worth reading. As much as my societal roots were a background and influence on me, so, too, has been my spiritual development.

Down through the years, it has been as if God has presented doors for me to open. As each door was presented to me, each opened and led me to an new awareness, a deeper connection, to the Spirit and Energy that is God, and the experiences that were opened up to me through this awareness. Throughout the rest of this book, you'll read about my experiences. However, I want to share with you the inspiration that is still the major part of my life and provided me with strength, down through the years.

As a young child, living on Lieb Street with our whole family, I thought of God as some great big white man up in the sky somewhere. That was early in my life, back when my family was attending Macedonia Baptist Church, and then as we moved on to Friendship Baptist Church.

My time at Friendship Baptist Church was special to me. I had been baptized there when I was ten years old. My Aunt Rosa Lee was in the senior choir and would take me with her. I'd march with her, in the choir, singing "Holy, Holy, Holy," to the choir loft, where I would sit next to her. The famous, Yolanda Maddox was the organist.

The Sunday school would put on annual Christmas plays and other holiday presentations. I remember when I was three years old, the Reverend J. H. Johnson picked me up and held me on the lectern, where I recited "Twas the Night Before Christmas."

God presented the first door to me when I was about ten years old. I had slipped into a coma-like state, and was hospitalized at Children's Hospital. I don't remember where I was when it happened, or how it was caused, but I do remember reviving from it. Consciousness returned to me when I was lying on a table, in a room full of people. All of them were dressed in white. They were medical students, observing me. And the instructing physician was Dr. Ossian Sweet. He was explaining to the students what was going on inside of me. So there he was, explaining to these students about whatever it was that had befallen upon me, and I woke up. Whatever medical magic he performed, I certainly did not understand it, but it made him famous. I considered it a miracle.

Dr. Sweet's accomplishments, however, were overshadowed by the criminal case he was involved in a number of years later. Dr. Sweet had moved into a house on Garland Street, east of Mack and the Boulevard. It was not a ritzy neighborhood, but it was a white neighborhood. And like many white neighborhoods at the time, no African American resident would be welcomed.

A crowd of about 300 had gathered outside of his newly purchased home. They were angry, hurling rocks at the home, in an attempt to chase him out. They didn't know that Dr. Sweet was also a hunter. He would go on hunting trips, bringing home additional food for meals. Either he or his brother, Henry, who was also in the home, retrieved one of the hunting rifles. Dr. Sweet warned the crowd that he would not be driven from his home. During the exchange, a white man sitting across the street on his porch, was shot and killed, and Dr. Sweet and his brother, Henry, were arrested and charged with murder.

This enraged the nation. The NAACP took to Dr. Sweet's defense, and brought in the famous attorney, Clarence Darrow. At trial, before an all-white jury, and Judge Frank Murphy, both Dr. Sweet and his brother were set free because the jury failed to reach a verdict. In a second trial, the prosecution tried only Henry Sweet, who had admitted to firing the gun. But with Darrow defending him, the all-white jury acquitted Henry.

My revival from this coma-like state opened a door for me. God must have delivered me from this state in some way. This prompted my young mind to begin asking questions. How did God know I was sick? Where is this God? Is he white or black?

I began to take a closer look at what was being taught to me, as I was becoming more involved in the church. I heard the hellfire and damnation stories that were taught, and tried to make sense of them. I witnessed and heard about people having experiences of God, through their prayers. I expected to have that kind of experience when I was baptized, but I only felt the cold water. I began praying, all the time, still seeking that experience, but didn't feel anything. I wondered why I couldn't feel God like other people could. I could feel something close to what they were describing when I sang. But I figured that I was going to have to work hard to see God.

Because of our move to Maple Street, while I was at Miller Intermediate School, my mother began taking me to Calvary Baptist Church. I remember politicians coming to the church and enlisting the children to pass out leaflets. They once gave me a sign to carry that read "Booze Won't Buy Shoes," during prohibition. This was my earliest recollection of political activism, where I came to understand that I could stand up for or against issues.

Calvary was very kind to me, because they gave me the opportunity to be active in a lot of ways. In fact, I was kept busy at the church all seven days of the week. On Monday night, we had Joshua Prayer Band. Mrs. Artellia W. Hutchins, who brought her daughter, Ruth Jean, directed us. Ruth Jean, Lela Wilcox, Roberta Smith and I were great friends during this time. Then on Tuesday night, we had junior church and choir rehearsal. On Wednesday night, there was a prayer meeting for the parents, and the children would accompany them. Thursday and Friday night we would travel with Reverend Thomas A. Dorsey throughout the city of Detroit, to perform the songs that he had written. He wrote some of the most famous gospel songs that we still sing today, like "Precious Lord Take My Hand," and others. This was an interesting time, because the songs that he composed were being considered a sinful violation of the old traditional music we had sung in church. We, as children, bore the brunt of some of the criticism, however we were well trained in singing, and it was a joy to travel about, singing Reverend Dorsey's gospel music. Ironic, too, that at the time, there was a big band leader named Thomas Dorsey. I remember the kids of that era dancing to the great jazz music of Thomas Dorsey on Saturday nights, then listening to or singing the gospel music of Reverend Thomas A. Dorsey on Sunday.

During the day on Saturday, we would meet at Mrs. Hutchins' home for evangelical Bible class. This would take place in the morning, and then we'd have the rest of the day to do secular things, like attend a movie.

I was also a Sunday school teacher when I was 14 years old, and was in charge of the vacation Bible school during the summer. This provided me with the awareness of the needs of young people. I would take children to Belle Isle to learn how to roller-skate and ride a bicycle. In the early morning, we would go with our tennis rackets, hoping to be allowed on the tennis courts. Of course, we were told that we couldn't, or were not allowed. Only the white children and adults were allowed to play on them. This was just another obstacle we faced growing up African American in a prejudicial era.

On the other hand, millions cheered Joe Louis' success. Joe Louis attended church at Calvary Baptist, and his mother was the head of the Lily of the Valley Club, which my mother belonged to. He was a superior, skilled boxer who was embraced by all of America. On the night of June 22, 1938, he faced Max Schmeling, who was a German. At the time, Hitler was in power in Germany, and was preparing for war. Schmeling came to New York, representing Nazi Germany, and as the only man who had defeated Joe Louis, which occurred two years prior. Joe had won the right to battle Schmeling again, for the heavyweight title. But the match had more global significance. American vs. German. African American vs. Nazi. The symbolism of the fight played on many levels. When Max Schmeling fell to the canvas after a two minute and four second barrage of Joe Louis punches, America erupted with joy.

I listened to the fight on the radio, and when it was over, my Aunt Maudie, her friend Henrietta, and I went down to Chene Street. The atmosphere was charged with jubilation. The business district of Detroit, which was all white-owned, littered the streets with toilet paper in celebration of Joe's victory. The businesses in the section of the city we were in, had ceased - shows, beer gardens, everything - because the people were in the streets cheering. Noise was made by people banging wooden spoons against pots and pans.

African Americans have faced many obstacles, like the denial of access to the tennis courts on Belle Isle. But when an African American achieved greatness on the level of what Joe Louis achieved, particularly against a representative of Nazi Germany, we were embraced.

Overcoming obstacles is something that African Americans are familiar with. Everyone – no matter the race or gender - has personal obstacles in which they, too, must hurdle. It may take time and persistence, but they can be overcome. Do not let your obstacles become barriers that prevent and block your way toward the greatness you wish to achieve.

*****

My involvement at Calvary went beyond singing in the choir and teaching vacation Bible school. I wanted to start a junior nurse's guild, to help promote good health to the church members. I approached the leadership at Calvary with this idea, and though they were apprehensive at first, they accepted the idea. They assumed that the program would be harmless, however I took matters beyond their expectations.

One of the major health issues at the time was syphilis and gonorrhea. So I brought Mrs. Pearl Collins, one of the first African American women hired by the health department of the City of Detroit, to the church. She candidly discussed these two diseases, and brought illustrations with her, to aid in her instruction. Well, there were church members that were about to throw me out for that. Fortunately for me, the majority tolerated it.

But we didn't stop there. We examined other issues that were health related. For example, the health department brought us a map that showed where the highest levels of tuberculoses occurred. As it turned out, it was highest within the African American community. I wanted to know why African Americans were more susceptible to tuberculoses, and discovered that there was no regular garbage collection by the City in the African American community, as there had been in other communities. Thus, disease was more prevalent. I further came to understand that city government was involved in this service, and that city services were not provided equally from neighborhood to neighborhood. The poor received much fewer services than others, and the quality of service depended upon the quantity of wealth within the neighborhood. This opened my eyes to see how city politics worked, and its potential for change. I wanted to clean up the City so we would not have tuberculoses that killed people because they were poor and couldn't fight back. Equal distribution of garbage service seemed like a simple solution that would end, or at least lessen, a life threatening health problem. It was a problem we could not tackle as junior nurses. However, our awareness of it, and communicating this knowledge to church members was something we felt was important.

I was personally hurt by Calvary Baptist leadership when I was around sixteen or seventeen years old, which caused me to leave them. Years prior to the Schmeling victory, Joe Louis had to go all the way to the Brewster Center to train. It was quite a distance from the church and neighborhood in which he lived. But the children idolized him, and followed him everywhere. So I had approached the leadership of the church, suggesting that they put some boxing equipment in the basement of the church, like punching bags and gloves, so that the children could practice and have fun, and where Joe could train and have a positive influence on the children. The leadership of the church told me that they would give the idea some consideration.

On Mother's Day, the reverend gave a sermon that brought tears to my eyes, and my mother's eyes. He preached about the degeneration of the youth, and their inappropriate behavior. He went on to condemn the notion that children would request boxing to be allowed in the sacred building of a church. My suggestion had been publicly turned down, condemning me (though not addressing me personally), as being a contributor to the degeneration of society. This struck me hard, and I sought spiritual and religious development elsewhere.

Today, Calvary Baptist Church still conducts services, of which I occasionally attend or speak at. Furthermore, under the direction of Pastor Foster, Calvary observes Erma Henderson Day, every year, where I also speak to the congregation on the third Sunday in July. The fond memories and my spiritual development at Calvary still outweighs the one negative incident of my adolescence.

Photo by Michael Kitchen

ERMA HENDERSON DAY
CALVARY BAPTIST CHURCH
JULY 16, 2000

*****

44

Just as a person's childhood is an important influence on who he or she becomes, I could not tell my story without also revealing the roots of my spiritual life. Understanding that my life has a spiritual basis, which developed from these roots, will help you to understand the story of my life. God is my life, and I have always tried to walk the spiritual path.

This is the case for everyone, including you. No matter what your childhood consisted of, it profoundly impacted who you are today, and the decisions you make in your life. So, too, does your spirituality. You may not attend a church or think about spirituality. You may attend a church as a matter of presentation to others, but not take to heart a life of spirituality. You may be a very serious spiritual seeker and practitioner. Regardless of the level, your spiritual beliefs and practice have a profound impact on the decisions you make in your life, and with your interaction with others.

I know that God is Spirit. And God is an individual affair. I must and do respect God in every living soul, no matter how the person acts or reacts to living on this planet. This Spirit can be found in everyone, and can be recognized as breath. Breath is life, for without it, the person is not alive. Where there is breath, there is God.

CHAPTER THREE
Young Republican

After I graduated high school in 1934, I had to find whatever work I could. Jobs were scarce, this during the depression. While I was in high school, I had worked at Neisner's Dime Store as a result of the salesmanship class that I had taken. I thought I could go to them for a job, but they weren't hiring. No one was hiring. I tried getting a job downtown, where the many department stores and office buildings would be willing to hire an African American in the position of a maid or elevator operator, but I was unsuccessful. Actually, I was the wrong color. The African Americans who did secure those jobs were of the fairest skin. In other words, to get a job, an African American had to look more "Caucasian" than "African."

So I became a self-employed person who did a lot of little jobs. I would write letters for the older people on the block, and obituaries whenever necessary. My home was a drop off point for the Detroit Tribune, the only African American newspaper in the city, and I made a few pennies selling copies. I was learning how to type, and became a notary public. My living room was my front office. They were challenging times for all of us, but particularly so for African Americans because so many doors of opportunities were closed to us. I wouldn't bring home more than $10 a week. Compared to a $5 a day job at Ford, money was tight.

I did a little babysitting for Mrs. Ketz's daughter, Shirley, which brought in a little more money. Mrs. Ketz was a Jewish woman who was married to a Canadian man. She worked at Kern's Department Store. Shirley was very young at the time, and we became quite fond of each other. I would play with her, feed her, and sometimes I would get to take her to the movie theater. Though after about a year, I became dissatisfied with babysitting, mainly because of an incident with Mrs. Ketz's brother. He was there one day while I was babysitting, and was causing me all sorts of trouble, both in asking me to do additional chores, such as washing the windows of their apartment, to being aggressively flirtatious. So I chose to end that employment.

Once, I responded to an advertisement in the newspaper for a housekeeping position. The house was on East Grand Boulevard, and it was beautiful. There was a fireplace both upstairs and downstairs. The first floor maid position was offered to me, which I accepted. I was to be paid $10 a week.

When I accepted, I didn't realize that cooking would be one of the job responsibilities. I was not the most adept at cooking. I could bake, as I had back in junior high school, and I could put together some home-style meals that were not the custom of this person's home. No, they were looking for very elegant and fancy meals to be coming out of their kitchen, which I was not accustomed to. Roast beef? Pork chops? These things I had never prepared.

After the third day of work, Mrs. Van Ziel, the woman I was working for, gave all the hired help in the house a party. I was invited. I was thrilled. But then she told me that she didn't think that I would work out. She thought it was too much work for me, and that I didn't look more than sixteen years old (I had just recently graduated high school, so I was a little older than that). She also explained to me that her husband, Judge Donald Van Ziel, had helped to write laws against child labor, and for that reason, they had to let me go. She was generous enough, however, to give me a full week's pay upon leaving.

Despite the economic challenges, we did ok. It was just the three of us - Mom, my younger sister Doris, and I - living in a beautiful home at 2700 Maple Street, at a rate of $50 a month for our section. The house gave me a sense of what it felt like to be wealthy, despite our actual income. Mother was working at Michigan Mutual Liability Hospital, and the earnings from my odd jobs contributed to the household. There was never any fear of where our next meal would come from, either. The landlord of our Maple Street home operated a vegetable stall at Eastern Market. Every Saturday, he invited us to come down and get groceries from his stall. We would take our little red wagon and fill it with cauliflower, lettuce, beets and bananas. Some of the bananas we would give to the family in the lower flat of our home.

Michigan Mutual Liability Hospital would also send my mother home with extra food that the doctors and nurses didn't eat on the job, which would spoil otherwise. We also had a pear tree behind our house, which bore fruit for us.

Because we had access to so much food, my mother would insist that we give some away. Every Sunday morning, around four or five o'clock, she would have Lela Wilcox and I go to the Rosebud Creamery and fill our red wagon with bottles of milk. We would then pull the wagon down from Antietum Street, where the Creamery was, to Calvary Baptist Church, on Clinton and Joseph Campeau. We'd leave the milk there for the church ladies to use, as they provided food for the poor out of the church's kitchen. In those days, that was a major contribution to a church.

*****

At this time, I entered the political world. Out of high school, I became active in the local Republican Party, and was elected to the board of the Appomattox Republicans Club of the 1st District. Onslow Parrish was the president at the time, and we met at 323 Erskine Street.

When I was nine years old, my mother had given me two books to read. She said that these two books would be the foundation for my studies in life. One of the books was "Up From Slavery - the Life of Booker T. Washington." The other was "The Life of Abraham Lincoln." Because it was Lincoln who had put an end to the institution of slavery, and because he was a Republican president, and because southern Democrats were still promoting and practicing segregation, African Americans, including myself, were initially drawn to the Republican party.

I became consumed with this organization and the work I did with it. The organization thought I was a good speaker, so I joined the speaker's team. I would travel with an African American girl from Chicago. This was a unique situation because they wanted young people of voting age - 21-years-old at that time - to reach out and convince the young voter to register to vote. I was younger than 21, and whether they knew it or not, they continued to have me speak. I would dress like an older girl, which was a costly proposition. I had to make installment payments for my clothes. But to wear clothes like a beautiful dress, matching shoes, and white gloves, opened a door for me to grow and develop speaking and organizing skills as I helped to raise the awareness of other young people and women on the issues of the day.

Also, from my board position, I was able to establish a women's auxiliary division. This women's division grew to include not only women from the 1st District, but from the Thirteenth, Fourteenth, and Fifteenth districts, too. The Fourteenth District was in a predominantly white area, around Mack Avenue.

We also organized an extension of the Red Cross by training the women of the Appomattox Republicans Club. Once or twice a year, we would hit the streets in our white dresses with red crosses, to make sure everyone was being taken care of. The Red Cross was segregated at the time, and though they didn't let us in their building to help with the collection of blood or other things to help the African American community, we wanted to do our part to help the community.

I spoke at many engagements, but there are a few of them that distinctly come to mind. One such engagement was when I was invited to speak at the Battle Creek Women's Club. I dressed myself up to look like a grown woman, and rode the bus out to the location. The hall had two young African American men flanking the front door. As I approached, they stopped me. They told me that I could not enter through the front door, but rather, I had to use the rear entrance, like all African Americans had. I respectfully declined the use of their customary procedure, and explained to them that I was the guest speaker invited by the lady hosting the luncheon. They still refused to allow me to enter, until one of them got the attention of the woman hosting the luncheon. She came out, and profusely apologized for my waiting at the front door. I was probably the first African American ever to have walked through the front door of that establishment. The speech went well, and the women expressed their appreciation in having me speak.

This was a common theme whenever I would be sent out to speak at engagements where the community was predominantly white Americans. Most of the people were good to me, despite the shock they experienced when they realized that an African American would be addressing them. I guess when they heard that a Republican woman named Erma Henderson was sent to speak, an African American is not what their imaginations conjured. Once the fact struck them, there seemed to be a kind of phoniness in their behavior. I was young, and this frustrated me, and I didn't know how to handle it. A Republican woman was going to speak to them. Why should it matter that I was African American? I decided to politely, but definitely, break down discrimination along the way, such as using the front door of an establishment. I chose to connect through our common goals as Republicans and women, to defeat prejudicial thinking.

That is how you can deal with any obstacle. Another is how we handled the Pantland Hotel in Grand Rapids, in 1938. You have to have a vision of what it is you are trying to achieve, and when an obstacle presents itself, only your heart and knowing that your vision is desirable and achievable will overcome the obstacle.

For example, the City of Detroit was lacking a Secretary of State's office in the African American community. Our Appomattox Republicans Club recognized this and sought a solution. To get a Secretary of State's office, we needed to petition the state legislature in Lansing. So, we took our cause to Lansing and voiced our need and desire to have a Secretary of State's office in the African American community in Detroit. Finally, in 1939, the State granted our organization, and other political groups from the area, the privilege of opening the first African American Secretary of State's office in Detroit. It was located on Verner Highway, close to Brush Street and Beaubien, and very close to Ed Davis' big automobile showroom. Ed Davis was the first African American to open an auto dealership in the city of Detroit. In fact, Davis provided so much business for license plate sales through our office, that we would bring him and his workers into the office to handle their concerns separately, rather than to have them wait in the long lines that were common. Fortunately, I was able to become a part-time clerk at the office. It helped me financially, but I still had to secure other work.

*****

The Appomattox Republicans Club's Women's Auxiliary received an invitation from the Midwest Women's Regional Convention, another Republican organization, in Michigan City. I brought the subject up in a meeting, and four of us (Mrs. Vaney, her daughter Fedora, Lucy Perry, and I) decided we would attend. We were not invited to speak, but rather, to attend as active Republicans. Two of the women were very dark skinned African Americans, and the other was slightly darker in complexion than me. In other words, we were definitely not white-looking women, and after the Pantland Hotel experience, it would be interesting to see the reception we'd receive.

We purchased our tickets and rode on a bus destined for Chicago, stopping at Michigan City on the way. We were expected by the organizers of this event, and were surprised to find a horse and carriage waiting to pick us up. It was exciting to ride in such grand style, which transported us to the front of a beautiful lodge where the convention was being held. The scenery was breathtaking. There were blue thatched cottages along Lake Michigan. Waves rolled against a white sandy beach. It felt like paradise.

We left the carriage and proceeded to the stairs leading up to the lodge. There was a committee of women waiting for us. They expressed great pleasure in seeing us there, and were willing to help us throughout the convention. I thought that this time, it was going to be different. After the Pantland Hotel incident, and other beliefs that I heard being expressed as Republican views, I was becoming concerned about whether I could continue to support the Party. Perhaps here, at Michigan City, something would occur to help reinforce my feelings, one way or the other.

We entered the lodge to check in, and something did occur that caused the warm reception and beautiful surroundings to chill. Standing at the front desk was Gerald L. K. Smith. At the time, he was one of the nation's most outspoken voices of prejudice. He was the founder of the Christian Nationalist Crusade, and sought an America that was isolationist and governed by evangelical Christians. He was gracious in welcoming us, but I didn't understand what a person like that was doing at the convention.

The woman who was presiding over the affair asked us if the cottage was okay to stay in, instead of the main building. The cottages provided cooking facilities, and we could prepare our own food there. As lovely and tempting as the cottages were, we requested to stay in the lodge. I felt it was important for us not to be segregated away from the lodge, if that was their underlying intent.

The four of us stayed and attended the entire convention. We were all disgusted by its agenda. It was clear that we were the only African Americans in the building, and their speeches demonstrated that they had not expected any African Americans to show. More prejudice. More negative rhetoric. I then understood why the notorious Gerald L. K. Smith was present.

When the convention concluded, Lucy Perry and Fedora returned to Detroit. Mrs. Vaney and I went on to Chicago, because she wanted to visit her cousins. This gave me the opportunity to meet the first African American city hall appointees in Chicago, including S. Adron Jordan, the city clerk.

David Reynolds was a member of the Appomattox Republicans Club in Detroit, and while in Chicago, I met his brother. He showed me around, introduced me to people in the political field. They were African Americans who were also Republicans. From this experience, I learned something. There were African Americans and women in the Republican party who were accepting and cooperative and genuinely good-hearted. The problem resulted from the people who were in control of the party. Their agenda and programs excluded African Americans. These were the people who would agree with and have someone like Gerald L. K. Smith speak.

*****

I remember becoming eligible to vote. I was able to register through our Republican Club's appointee, Theodore White, at City Hall. I had been doing all this political work for four or five years, without the right for me to vote. But this was an exciting day for me. I was not yet 21 years old when I filled out the registration. And when Theodore White asked me to swear that the registration form stated the truth, I was discouraged, because I could not say that it was. He looked at me and said, "Now Erma, let's start over. Will you read this line. It clearly says that you are swearing that you are going to be twenty-one years old after you register, but before you vote. Isn't that true?" I was relieved, and signed the paper, and swore to it.

The power to vote is something, I feel, Americans take for granted, particularly young Americans. It is a power that gives you an expression to state who you are, and what you feel is important for us to move towards collectively as a society. I believe firmly that the voters are in charge of the destiny of the city, the state, and the nation, and if you fail to vote, you are turning over the city, the state, and the nation, to those who do vote.

At the same time, I wanted to become more involved in the election process, and decided to run for precinct delegate. The incumbent delegate was Mr. Edison, who had held the office for twelve years, and he would run again, though this time, I would be his toughest opponent. I campaigned throughout my entire district, going door to door, talking to everyone I could. This included German Americans, Polish Americans, and Italian Americans, all of them fluent in the tongue of their homeland. But I communicated with them, and explained to them the importance of casting their vote, and how to get to the polls on Election Day.

I also spoke to the issues within our precinct. One issue involved the closing of a juvenile detention center. It was located in the middle of the block within a neighborhood. The building became a central office for teachers in the district. However, every day, after they parked their cars, they locked the gates, and the neighborhood children could not get to the playground area, losing a place to play. The issue of regular garbage collection in the African American community became my concern, which was something that I had recalled from my Junior Nurses Guild days at Calvary Baptist Church.

Election day was very special to me. It was the first time that I could vote, and I was on the ballot as a precinct delegate. I was also working the polls, greeting many of the people who I had seen on my door-to-door campaign. In their heavy accents, they would say, "Oh Miss Erma, I'm going to mark for you, I'm going to mark for you." Well, Mr. Edison did not serve the next term. The people within my precinct district voted me into my first office.

*****

My desire to be involved with the Republican Party, however, was diminishing. Many factors concerned me, such as the conference in Michigan City, and the appearance of Gerald L. K. Smith. Such as witnessing wealthy white Republican young men stealing silverware at conferences. Such as hearing the Democrats, particularly in the South and the programs of President Franklin Delano Roosevelt, as they were taking action against bigotry and racism, while people within the Republican Party stood silent. I had read a book written by Wendell Wilkie called "One World," which showed me that people within communities all over the world, were not being taken care of. None of the Republican ideas or programs had a focus on bettering the conditions of all the people in society.

I had also become interested in the emergence and development of unions within industry. Throughout my life to that point, I had become acquainted with people who had moved up to Detroit from the South to gain employment in the automotive industry. I listened to people tell me about the purpose of unionism.

They provided clear pictures of its importance to provide better working conditions for all workers. An individual employee that would demand a better condition or better wage would find himself fired. But as a collective bargaining unit, the company would have to come to terms and conditions that were best for all of its employees.

So I was becoming involved with friends and neighbors who worked for Ford. I would remind them of the Sunday meetings at the union hall, or help find places to conduct meetings that would help to organize the unions, like churches and the basement of people's homes.

There was a man by the name of Monroe Lucky, who was part of Ford Local 600. He was a big guy, maybe weighing as much as 300 pounds, who told me that the way I spoke, I should be speaking at Cadillac Square, where all the union organizers would meet and make speeches. So one day, I went down there. It was quite a scene, with men standing on trucks or wagons, promoting unionism. I saw Monroe, and he encouraged me. I told him that I wasn't going to be able to get up on one of those trucks. The big man that he was, he lifted me up, and I suddenly found myself standing on the hood of one, overlooking a crowd of people. I looked down at him and asked, "What do you want me to say?" He told me to tell the people why they should join and support a union.

So that's what I did. I just spoke. They weren't used to hearing a woman speak, so they paid me some attention. I talked about why I was leaving the Republican Party, and supported the growth and development of unions. I finished, and found myself suddenly immersed in support and acceptance.

As you can imagine, this ideological shift removed me from the Republican Party. It was a difficult move for me. I had wonderful experiences and friends while developing the four districts of women for the Appomattox Republicans Club. But President Roosevelt's programs earned my respect, and the growth of unionism had great potential for the benefit of all working people, that I had to break away from my involvement with the Republican Party.

Eleanor Roosevelt was also an inspiration. She was the type of woman who gave you hope and courage to do things. I remember her visit to the Brewster Project, where she walked and talked within this African American community. When I heard that she was there, I rushed to get to where she was, but the crowd was too large for me to get anywhere near her. I was inspired by her work and by her speeches. She and Mary McLoud Bethune were leading women of the time. Both women would electrify the crowd wherever they went. Mary McLoud Bethune developed schools for African Americans, particularly in the South, and became an advisor to President Roosevelt on minority issues.

Eleanor was devoted to women's issues, and women's needs, no matter what the race. She desired justice and freedom for all. Yet, she also had the strength to help the President, who was crippled with polio. The final work of their era was the development of the United Nations, which Eleanor was very involved in. She co-authored the Universal Declaration of Human Rights, and served as a United Nations delegate from 1945-1953, and again in 1961. I would give them credit to being two of the most outstanding people of my era.

*****

This was a period of time in my life that I was also a married woman.

My friend, Lela Wilcox, married George Burnett Jr., a boy I had known since I was about three or four years old. This occurred shortly after we graduated from high school. As I was becoming active in causes and political issues, my friends were getting married.

Lela's mother was very fond of me. She spent a lot of money on Lela's wedding dress, and afterwards, she approached me and said that she would have the dress taken up and she'd give it to me for my wedding day. I was very honored and touched. However, marriage wasn't on my mind at all. Especially because I wasn't involved with any men at the time! I had several male friends, and a few that I was charmed by. But I wasn't in love with any of them, which is why I stayed the course of dedicating my life to issues and causes.

One day, I was walking by the Caplan Theater, and passed a barber shop where I knew the guys who worked there. I decided to drop in to say hello. There, I met this fine young man. George Henderson was his name. He was a nice, clean-cut guy. We hit it off immediately, and began dating shortly thereafter. I eventually met his family, and they warmly accepted me. After a period of time together, we decided that we would get married.

The ceremony was at my mother's home, on September 25th, 1935. Preston Foster was our violin soloist. He was a musical genius. I wore Lela's dress. The house was filled with family, friends, and neighbors. There was such an outpouring of love from the church and the people that it truly made for a special day. My cousin, Hazel Lymon, who later married the famous attorney, Charles Roxborough, gave us a silver tray as a gift. It was the most auspicious gift and was the talk of the reception. This blessed event, during the midst of the Depression, made the silver tray that much more extravagant.

George and I settled into an apartment on Chene Street. It was on the upper floor, up a tall, steep staircase. The view was beautiful. And this is was how my name changed from Erma McQueen to Erma Henderson.

*****

I was at just a kid at the time, just over 18 years old. George was ten years older than I. I believe I was swept into the glow of wanting to be married like my girlfriends. I was in love with being in love. It didn't take us long to realize the differences in our interests. I was actively involved with the Republican Party, and was beginning to develop an interest in the union movement. I was also becoming bored with trying to become a wife. My trips across the state did not include George because he was not interested in such things. Then, my personal support of the Republican Party began to diminish. I think George noticed this, and encouraged me to get more involved with the unions.

And so I did. It did not take long afterwards that our marriage came to an end. George and I discovered that our relationship worked better being friends, rather than as husband and wife. I was too young to know really what love was, and too ambitious for change in the community to settle down and be a housewife. When we decided to end our marriage, we did so in a friendly manner. I moved back in with my mother.

After we had separated, George was called to war. My mother, Aunt Maude, my sister, and I, had moved to a four room apartment at 77 East Canfield, leaving the old neighborhood, so we would be closer to where I was working on East Warren, at Great Lakes Mutual Insurance Company. It was at that time that George and I had to officially get a divorce. On August 10, 1940, we filed the paperwork, and on February 19, 1941, our divorce was finalized.

Even though the marriage had ended, I retained the last name of Henderson, for convenience. In those days, women would establish credit in their husband's name. If they returned to their maiden name after a divorce, they would have to re-establish credit. Therefore, in order to avoid fighting over my ability to purchase something on credit, I kept his last name.

George and I have remained friends down through the years. His family is still my family. He married a woman named Thelma shortly after returning home from World War II, and they have become a part of my family, too. His daughter, Emma, was very close to me when I was on Detroit City Council. In fact, when I was ordained as a minister at the Divine Temple of Mental Science, Thelma and Emma showed up. They also visited my health food store. They have supported me in my campaigns, and they would go on the boat rides and bring friends when we were raising money for the campaign. I love them still today, as family.

CHAPTER FOUR
The 1940's

The 1940's was a period of growth for me. I had long since left Calvary Baptist Church, and was seeking new answers to who God was, and how could He knew so much. This journey led me to the teachings of Eric Butterworth and the Unity movement.

Eric Butterworth was on the radio every day, and I would listen to his message. I then learned he was speaking at the Detroit Institute of Arts every Sunday morning, so I would occasionally attend. The teachings intrigued me because of its focus on practical spirituality. It called on me to practice my spiritual belief. Previously, the message from the church was "do what I tell you to do." I was not required to use my mind. Unity provided me with a new approach, one where I had to use my mind, because my mind was a tool for God. The other churches taught that people would pray for you and you were saved or you were healed. It all came from outside your self. Unity was teaching that you had the power to use your mind to develop anything inside yourself spiritually. When I first discovered Unity, I was still young at the time, just out of high school, in my late teens. It was quite a new way of experiencing God.

*****

Though I had been listening to Eric Butterworth and had read other Unity and metaphysical material, I was introduced to my spiritual teacher as she stood by my bedside.

I had become ill. This illness, again, caused me to lapse into a state of unconsciousness. My mother had me examined by three doctors, and each of them wanted to do exploratory surgery. They could not figure out what was wrong with me. But my mother refused them. She was against the idea of cutting me open without knowing why they were cutting, or what they were looking for. I remained in this comatose state for three days.

When I did regain consciousness, my eyes opened to see a woman sitting next to my bed. She was dressed in white. "Are you an angel?" I asked. She smiled, then asked me if I was hungry. I said I was. My Aunt Maude entered the room, and became quite ecstatic. The woman directed her to get me a piece of toast.

As we waited for the toast, the woman introduced herself as Reverend Ann Ryan. She had been sitting with me during my coma. My Aunt Maudie had attended a church where Reverend Ryan had spoken. Impressed by her talk, Aunt Maudie approached Reverend Ryan and told her about my illness. So there she was, sitting in the room with me, a complete stranger, praying for me, waiting for me to return to a conscious state. I instantly wanted to know more about her.

Reverend Ann Ryan recommended that I take regular healing "treatments" at her home. I objected to this, because she lived so far away. I could get to her home only if I took a streetcar. I really didn't like riding the streetcar. But she asked me, "What is riding a street car to you?" She said that I would ride the street car every week, and the day will come when I would no longer worry about riding a street car, that, in fact, I would eventually drive a car of my own, and also soar around the world.

On every Saturday of that summer, I rode the streetcar, to receive healing treatments from Reverend Ryan. I was so impressed with this woman. As I got to know her, she'd tell me what I was thinking and tell me what I needed to know and how to proceed in life.

I learned a great deal about spirituality from her. She taught me that God is not a man, nor a woman. God is spirit. Reverend Ryan would say to me "Spirit is the breath of God. Intangible, but you can feel it. When God is working through you, you can feel the Spirit working through you for good. If you don't feel that spirit working with you all the time, you're open for the possibility of evil to come through your mind. Thoughts like envy, jealousy, or revenge could take over." It was a turning point for me. God is not a Spirit, but rather, God is Spirit.

Photographer unknown

REVEREND ANN RYAN

*****

I was working at Great Lakes Mutual Insurance Company, where I met the president of the company, Charles H. Mahoney, and his wife, Lula. They were middle-aged, and had married as childhood sweethearts. He was a brilliant man, an attorney who had worked on the Sweet case I had mentioned earlier. He had broken the color barrier at a large law firm on Gratiot Avenue, which eventually led to his becoming president of Great Lakes Mutual Insurance Company.

Both he and Lula treated me like family. In fact, I called them Uncle Charles and Aunt Lu. They would take me up to the Great Lakes Country Club, a beautiful resort that was located somewhere between Pontiac and Flint, for summer vacations. Great Lakes Insurance owned the property. The water and scenery was refreshing, and there were lovely cottages that we stayed in. I spent about four vacation periods there with them.

However, Uncle Charles was living in fear, for he had had a heart attack. They had not been attending a church at the time. I had been reading Unity and other metaphysical teachings, was learning how to meditate, and studying truth teachings from Reverend Ryan. I would talk to them about what I had learned, and they would listen to me. I would tell them that they needed to change their thinking, because they wouldn't even go on a vacation for fear of not returning due to his heart. They had considered taking a trip to Mexico, but again, he was afraid that he would not come back alive, and so they almost decided not to. Through what I had learned by studying Unity principles, I was convinced that a person could use their mind to ascend to great heights, just as one could use their mind to maintain the same level of life experiences, or even to sink to the deepest depths of despair. Uncle Charles was a lawyer who handled all kinds of powerful cases. I explained to him that he could use the power of positive thinking to envision what it was he wanted to do. He could see himself planning for the vacation, and coming home from the vacation, healthy and wealthy and ready to go on to the next thing. I convinced them that God would work a miracle through him, through his mind, which would allow him to have a safe and enjoyable trip. So Uncle Charles started doing this, and he and Aunt Lu began to see the power of high visionary thinking. Then, together, they went to Mexico, and returned, and had had a wonderful time.

This was important to me. It was a religious experience for me to have been able to pass this message on to Uncle Charles and Aunt Lu. This developed credibility and confidence in what I was learning as well as my ability to practice it. These people I dearly loved. To have used my persuasive powers to convince someone that I loved and respected, like Uncle Charles, who was already a leader and intelligent person, to have more faith in himself through God and the power of his own mind, strengthened my own belief in what I was learning.

Uncle Charles and Aunt Lu became more involved in metaphysical study, which included joining a group that was studying the teachings of Mary Eadie Baker. Uncle Charles was later appointed by the government to an administrative position within the Navy, which caused them to move to New York City. There, he had another experience that demonstrated the power of the mind. His office had a beautiful view of the New York harbor. One day, while in his office, he made an off-handed comment, with coworkers nearby, about how beautiful it would be to see Navy ships passing through the harbor. The very next day, a Navy Commander entered his office and told him, "Your wish is our command, sir." Uncle Charles turned around and looked out of his window. There, in the New York harbor, were a number of the Navy's ships passing through. He had a vision of the fleet in the harbor, verbally put it out into the universe, and it manifested.

In New York, Aunt Lu became a leader and teacher of metaphysical studies. I missed them, but remember them fondly as two very influential people in my life.

*****

Yes, these were busy times for me. I was involved in helping the growth of automobile unions, working at Great Lakes Mutual Liability Insurance Company for Charles and Lula Mahoney, and had moved to 77 East Canfield, an apartment next door to a police station. I also began my involvement with the Elks.

The Improved Benevolent Protective Order of Elks of the World was founded in 1899. From this emerged the Daughters of the Elks, which was founded by Emma V. Kelly, whose daughter Vuena Kelly was the Grand Secretary. Under the direction of J. Finley Wilson, the "Grand Patriarch," Leah Wilson, his wife, who was head of the publicity department and was the Grand Organizer of the Daughter of the Elks, and Grace Bryant, who was the Michigan President of the Elks, I established Lady Camille Temple No. 755, in April of 1943. Our focus was the education of African American young people, with our guiding principles being charity, justice, sisterly and brotherly love.

ERMA L. HENDERSON
Founder
First Daughter Ruler
Former: Natl. Asst. Directress
Civil Liberties
Present: District Deputy

Photographer unknown

PHOTO OF ME FROM A LADY CAMILLE TEMPLE FLYER

In order to establish this chapter, I promised Elks leadership that I would have 100 women go through the initiation and become Elks, which I did. Every member who was on the original charter was present, with the exception of our chaplain, Reverend Ann Ryan. She had to excuse herself from the organization because she was on a mission of her own. According to her, God had instructed her to follow a three-part path. First, she was to rent a church, and conduct metaphysical teachings within. Second, as the membership grew, she was to buy a building to house the church, which eventually she did on St. Aubin Street. Finally, she was to build a church, a new structure and building from which to teach from. Because of this three-step process, Reverend Ryan was teaching on Tuesday nights, which was the designated night for our meetings. Even though she could not attend, I left her listed on our original charter, as our chaplain.

To help African American youths broaden and improve their minds, we held oratorical contests. These contests would begin at the temple level, then a winner would advance to a local area level, then on to a state level, then on to a regional level, which finally led to a national contest, which would entitle the winner to a $1,000 scholarship to be paid to the college that the winning child would attend. Many good people participated in these contests, including my godson, Dr. Arthur Carter, who went as far as the regional level. These oratorical contests brought the best out of individuals, who became powerful and active members in their communities. Dr. Martin Luther King Jr. was a national winner of one of these oratorical contests. We held these contests on the property of the various Elks lodges and temples that had been purchased, so that there was no issue as to whether we, as African Americans, were allowed to rent a space for such an occasion.

So this was a busy period for me. Besides directing the Lady Camille Temple, I was making the grand sum of $13 per week at Great Lakes Mutual

Insurance Company, and helping the growth of unions, even though I was having a difficult time being accepted by union people because I was working for a business and was not a union member myself.

*****

The area of the city known as Paradise Valley was beginning to boom. This was the major business and entertainment district in the African American community. Hotels like the Gotham Hotel, Carver Hotel, and Sunnie Wilson's Mark Twain Hotel provided fine accommodations for guests to the city. The Garfield Lounge, the Chocolate Bar, and the Forest Club, among others, provided night spots where famous entertainers, like Billie Holiday, would perform. There were theaters along Hastings Street. All of these were thriving African American owned businesses, and were fine establishments. The Forest Club, at Forest and Hastings, had a roller rink, meeting hall, and bowling alley, housed the longest bar in town at 107 feet, and was larger than the old Madison Square Garden in New York City. There were African American churches in the neighborhood, including Reverend C.L. Franklin's Bethel Baptist Church on Hastings. His daughter, Aretha Franklin, and her sister, Erma, sang in the church choir there. The whole area was alive with activity as the community grew and developed its economic base.

I was very fortunate to have my job at Great Lakes Mutual Insurance Company, but in order to survive I had to take on two other jobs. One of them was to do evening work for attorney Gerald L. Dixon. He was on the staff of the Unemployment Compensation Commission, and would handle private cases after hours, for which he needed a secretary. I would go over to his home and utilize and refine my secretarial skills.

My other job was working for the Twelve Horseman's Club. On a part-time basis, I would help them produce a membership list, which the state required clubs to maintain in order to keep their liquor license.

The Phoenix Club was a Jewish response to the Detroit Athletic Club's discrimination. The Detroit Athletic Club's bylaws included a prohibition of African American and Jewish members. Therefore, Jewish members of the community developed the Phoenix Club. The Twelve Horsemen's Club, similarly, accepted only African American and Jewish members.

So between these three jobs and my other activities, I discovered the stress relieving benefits of massage. The physical drain of working three jobs in order to cover rent and family expenses did become overwhelming. I discovered Brady's Health Studio, and every Friday I would spend three dollars out of my pay for a quick wash down and rub down. It was a rough kind of massage, not like the finer, more trained massage we have today. As tight as money was, I still had no problem paying three dollars to physically rejuvenate and remove the stress from my body and life.

*****

I was eventually promoted from being a clerk to that of head of the policy department, bringing my pay up to $85 per month. But that was still low in comparison to the union positions that were opening up to women in the factories, due to World War II. I began weighing whether I should stay working three jobs, or look for a factory position. At Great Lakes Mutual Insurance Company I could advance no further. So I began looking for another job, and found one with the Federal Public Housing Authority.

I was hired to be a typist, but I was assigned to operate the Teletype. It was to be my exclusive responsibility. However, I would be given other tasks to perform, such as writing travel vouchers for employees who were traveling on business, to being a messenger to get paperwork to other parts of the city. It was also the first job that allowed me to become a union member.

Because I was given assignments that were outside my job description, I took my complaint to Colonial Hollenback, the Federal Regional Director of the Midwest Region. His office was located in Chicago, but he would occasionally come to Detroit. After listening to my complaint, he thought I might be a good director of a housing project. He then sent for Paul. Paul was an African American man who drove the housing department van. Colonial Hollenback instructed Paul to take me out to Ecourse and River Rouge, to a housing project that was being constructed. It was a long drive, and when we arrived, I realized I couldn't take this position. I did not have a car that I could drive, and, for that matter, I did not know how to drive. I didn't want to have to depend upon Paul or anyone else to drive me out to that location every day.

I rejected the position. Because of this, Colonial Hollenback ignored my complaints. This led me to become a union member. I approached Irving Riskin, the union representative for the United Office and Professional Workers of America (UOPWA), which represented office employees, including those who worked for the Federal Public Housing Authority, and he had me sign up. I received my own union card. In the evenings, I would walk to the union hall on Griswold Street to see what other kinds of jobs were posted and available.

But this led me to more discrimination. For when I would go to the union hall after work, I would meet other women there, and we'd chat. Sometimes, our conversations were engaging enough that we would go across the street to a restaurant for coffee. The women were Caucasian, and I was the only African American amongst them. When the waitress came to serve the group, she would take the orders of the white women, and bring them their coffee, while completely ignoring me. Some nights, I would stay in my seat until the restaurant closed, and only then would they serve me. Some nights, they would completely refuse to serve me, and would call the police to have them order me to leave. Eventually, the other women refused to frequent this restaurant because of the discrimination, and once it began to hurt business, the restaurant changed its policy.

Then, the Twelve Horsemen Club purchased the Phoenix Club, and the Twelve Horsemen Civic Center was about to open. I was still working at the club, helping them with their membership list and performing other odd jobs. The management approached me and asked me if I would accept the position of Director of the Twelve Horsemen Civic Center. For this position, I left the Federal Public Housing Authority.

*****

The Twelve Horsemen Civic Center was a luxurious facility. It had a huge kitchen in the basement equipped to serve meals for large groups that would utilize the banquet hall on the second floor. On the first floor, there were a number of rooms for relaxing and engaging in conversation. One was a bar. The others we individually named, like the Palm Room, the Red Room, and the Blue Room. The second floor was where the offices were, including my office. There was also a handball court that we converted into an auditorium and ballroom. The renovation that took place to make this change was the first time I had seen an African American contractor granted a job. It made me feel so proud, because it symbolized to me that African Americans were on the road to success.

I loved this job. I was earning more than I had been at Great Lakes Mutual and at the Federal Housing Commission. As far as location goes, it was perfect. It was within a short walking distance of my home on Canfield Street. Lady Camille Temple of the Daughters of the Elks was located at 69 Erskine, the Twelve Horsemen Club was at 323 Erskine, and the Twelve Horsemen Civic Center was at 114 Erskine. Everything I was involved in was within a short distance for me.

The job also provided me with the opportunity to develop the Civic Center into anything I wanted it to be. It gave me great creative freedom. I was able to hire my Aunt Maudie to tend to the coat check room, and I employed two secretaries. I became skilled at preparing and catering wedding receptions. There was a private nightclub on the first floor, which, during World War II, served as a canteen for African American service people when they were in town on leave. The ballroom was one of the major ballrooms for African Americans in the city. Famous and talented musicians and bands performed in the nightclub, which would create a line of patrons that circled the block. Occasionally, people would dance until one o'clock in the morning, and I'd be with them, only to return for work the next morning. It was rough, but it was worth it. I loved being involved with the people.

For our special events in the ballroom, I would contact Edgar Brazelton of Brazelton's Flowers. He was an African American florist on Brush Street, who later moved to West Grand Boulevard, where his florist shop is well known. Weddings, banquets, church and union events were that much more elegant and special with Brazelton's Flowers' touch.

I remember training the waitresses that worked there. Someone had questioned my knowledge and experience at being a waitress, and I responded that I knew how I liked to be served, and that was the only experience I needed.

One night, my creativity was put to task. There was an organization that had rented the upper ballroom for a huge banquet. During that day, however, the dumbwaiter, which would transport the food from the kitchen in the basement, to the hall on the second floor, had broken. This was an emergency situation, for I needed the food prepared in the kitchen and taken to the ballroom for the banquet. My chef, who was an outstanding Canadian chef, was frustrated at the thought of his food being cold by the time it would arrive on the guests' tables, and that would reflect negatively on him. I called the Twelve Horsemen's Club seeking advice and explained the situation. I was told to figure something out. An idea suddenly occurred, and I asked them if I could hire people for the evening. They agreed.

I then took to the streets. I found people who were unemployed, some who were destitute, and offered them five dollars for an evening's work. Most agreed. I rallied up my small army and marched them to the health club, where they took hot baths and shaved. Meanwhile, I gathered up all the white coats I could find, and had them ready for the men when they emerged from the showers. They were allowed to wear their own pants, but they all had to wear a white suit coat, making them look like a team. I then had them form a line from the kitchen, up two flights of stairs, to the ballroom, and instructed them on their assignment for the evening. Simply, they were a human dumbwaiter. As the food was ready for serving, the tray would be handed to the first person, and passed along the line until it arrived at the last person upstairs in the ballroom, who then gave it to the server.

My chef was relieved when he understood the plan, and he regained his enthusiasm to perform his culinary artistry. Every dish arrived hot and on time. The whole evening proceeded without a flaw or complaint from the organization that rented our facility.

From this event, I came to realize a gift I had that I did not know I had. I had the ability to develop innovative ideas on the spur of the moment. And I know now, that this is how God works. God always provides a way, and that way can be found by being open and receptive to it. Whether the experience was the broken dumbwaiter or any other event in my life, I have been blessed by being open to find a way to accomplish something when, on the surface, it looked to be difficult.

*****

I offered other organizations the use of the Twelve Horsemen Civic Center as their meeting place. The AFL-CIO would hold a meeting every Wednesday. They required extra chairs, so their fee for the room was the cost of renting the chairs. The National Negro Labor Congress met there. There was another labor group or two that would meet at the Civic Center, which caused some of the members of the Civic Center to question whether labor groups should be allowed to meet at the Civic Center. Their concern was that the labor organizations members were predominantly white. This created some tension between myself and the membership of the Civic Center. I took to heart their concern, but in the end, I stood my ground. Labor organizations were being denied access to, and prohibited from meeting at other buildings. The unions, I felt, needed to become a positive and strong force, and to do so, they needed a stable center from which to meet and communicate with each other. Secondly, it was an opportunity to break the ice between the white community and the African American community. For these reasons, the Board of Directors backed my decision to allow labor unions access to our facility to hold their meetings.

I also held space at the Civic Center for the newsboys. I helped train the boys to deliver the Michigan Chronicle, like I had the Detroit Tribune back when I was working out of my home on Maple Street. The center became a dropping point for the newspapers, and the boys would pick them up and deliver them from that location. Neither the Civic Center nor I made any money from this, for it was a community service activity sponsored by the Civic Center.

I also earned the respect and support of Reverend Charles Hill, who was pastor of the Hartford Avenue Baptist Church. He would lead meetings of the NAACP in the Civic Center, from his position as president.

I was very involved with the NAACP, particularly in the fight against restaurant discrimination. Under the direction of Reverend Hill, we would form picket lines around restaurants that refused to serve African Americans. We demanded to be served, even though we were afraid of what the cooks or restaurant owners would do to the food that they served to us. Oftentimes, though, the police would be called in to order us to move on.

The struggle was difficult because each person involved in it was most likely holding a job or two and would have a family to take care of, while engaging in the battles necessary to create positive change.

One battle that was waged was for the Sojourner Truth housing project on the corner of Nevada and Ryan. The Detroit Housing Commission had sought to undertake the building of two housing projects; one for the African American community, the other for the white community. However, the federal government denied funding for two sites, and sought, instead, to develop a single building that would be for African American occupancy, within a white community. The white community was outraged by this, and because of the pressure put on Washington, the federal government changed its position, granting the Sojourner Truth Housing Project to the white community, in the early days of January in 1942. Reverend Hill led a coalition of Detroit citizens to demonstrate against the moral breach of the government's promise to the African American community. Again, the federal government changed its mind, and set the last day of February as the day African Americans could begin moving in.

This sparked a massive protest as thousands of white Detroiters barred entrance to the project by the new African American tenants. A riot ensued, which police battled for several hours. Thankfully, there were no deaths, however several people were injured. We marched around the building, in protest. National leaders arrived to help, such as Hopson R. Reynolds, who was the head of the civil liberties department of the Elks; the great Paul Robeson, the entertainer; and Adam Clayton Powell, a member of the United States House of Representatives. They delivered inspiring speeches, and drew great crowds and attention to our cause against prejudice and discrimination. The unions also participated and helped.

Eventually, we were able to get the federal government to enforce its commitment of housing to the African American community, without further violence.

But this was just the beginning, as racial tensions grew. The City's population continued to grow, and Southerners, both African American and Caucasian were moving to Detroit for its manufacturing jobs. Living space was vanishing and people found themselves in a very crowded environment.

It was June 20, 1943, when thousands of people filled Belle Isle for recreational purposes. The summer heat combined with the close proximity of fellow residents who were not of the same shade of skin, triggered interracial fights. A false rumor spread to the African American community, that white males had thrown an African American female and her baby over the Belle Isle Bridge and into the Detroit River. By midnight, interracial incidents erupted in Paradise Valley and along Woodward Avenue.

We lived next door to the police station, and I remember the inhuman display from my second floor window. There was a police wagon, its engine running, waiting for a police officer to put his prisoner inside. His prisoner was a thin, frail, old African American woman. The police officer, a large, white man, led her to the wagon, kicking her along the way.

I couldn't stand watching it any further. I started for the stairs when my mother screamed, "Don't go! Don't go down there. You can't interfere with the police. They've got guns." But I ran down the stairs, and rushed out of our home, shouting at the officer to leave the woman alone. But before I could get there, the officer lifted the old woman into the wagon, and kicked her inside. He climbed in behind her and closed the doors. As the wagon pulled away, I was left standing there, screaming and hollering. My mother was yelling for me to come back into the house and upstairs. Feeling helpless, I did so, crying and weeping because of the cruelty I had just witnessed. I did not know who the woman was, so there was no way I could ever find out if justice was ever served.

And there was little justice that resulted from this riot. The violence continued for two days, as federal troops were brought in to restore order. The numbers are horrendous. Thirty-four people were killed, of which twenty-five were African American. Seventeen of the twenty-five African Americans were killed by the police, yet no Caucasians died at the hands of the police. More than 1800 were arrested, though only 1182 were formally charged. Of those formally charged, 970 were African American.

I was appalled at the massive and ugly face of injustice, which reinforced my commitment to fight any form of injustice that emerged.

*****

I had a conversation with Uncle Charles - Charles Mahoney, from Great Lakes Insurance Company - about my going to college. I explained to him that I did not have the money for it, and wanted to know if he knew of any grants or scholarships that might be available. He said that he would speak to John Dancy, the president of the Urban League. He then set up an appointment for me to talk with him. When I arrived to meet with Mr. Dancy, he was able to secure a $100 grant from the Urban League to attend school.

So I left my position at the Twelve Horseman Civic Center to begin my first term at Detroit Institute of Technology. I really did not have the extra money to go to school. I felt as if I abandoned a good job, but I did not know of any other way to improve my opportunities for advancement without further education. And, as usual, I was extremely involved in life. I was developing Lady Camille Temple. I was active in Reverend Dr. Ann Ryan's church, as she was on the first step of her path, having rented a building to practice her ministry of metaphysical science. I was still engaged in the union effort, speaking wherever I was asked. I had also become a speaker on African American history.

My interest in African American history started when I was a child. I collected little newspaper clippings from the Pittsburgh Courier - one of the only African American newspapers at the time, along with the Detroit Tribune. J. A. Rogers created a little informative cartoon piece, similar to Robert Ripley's Believe It or Not cartoon, which depicted moments in African American history. I would collect and study these nuggets of information. I also had attended lectures at the YWCA on African American history that were presented by an African American history writer.

As I began conversing about African American history, I eventually would be asked to speak in homes, churches, and halls, especially during the month of February - African American History Month. I would even walk into businesses, like beauty shops, and spend a few minutes talking to the customers and beauticians about African American history, if they wanted to listen.

Though all this kept me busy, money was tight. I had to seriously consider putting off my education, and find a job.

*****

As I have said, as long as I stayed open to the possibility, God would provide a solution. A woman named Bridgett, who was a friend of mine visiting from London, told me about an opening at the National Maritime Union. I pursued it, and got the job. Not only was the pay good, but my scheduled shift to work was in the evenings, so I did not have to stop attending school. My classes were during the day, and I'd work in the evening.

The job, itself, was very simple. I had to run mimeograph copies of the labor contracts that the union had with the big companies that sailed their vessels on the Great Lakes. The union was bargaining and represented the seamen. I had to see to it that these contracts were copied and that each seaman would have a copy when their vessel had docked.

Norma Hanna was the port secretary when she hired me. She eventually left the position for a job in New York, which allowed Ruth Bellmont to fill her space. Shortly after her promotion, Ruth left the job for another position, and suddenly I found myself in the position of being the first African American woman to hold the port secretary position for the National Maritime Union AFL-CIO. This put the responsibility of the office on my shoulders. My supervisors were Charlie Monroe and Allen Durhall. Charlie did a lot of traveling throughout the state, and Allen's focus was more on conducting business with other companies.

I met and worked with seamen from all over the world, which continued my connection to and interest in international affairs. Growing up in an international neighborhood prepared me well for treating each person, no matter where they came from, as my brother. Some of the men became father figures to me, when docked during one of their regular stops in Detroit. These men unequivocally accepted me; in fact, I received, on average, a marriage proposal each week. The Greeks, especially, accepted me. There was a Greek restaurant downstairs in the building where I worked, and the men always made room for me to come down and have breakfast with them. Some of the men would bring me gifts from their ship, like canned food or perfume they bought in France. They would never give it to me, directly, but rather, slip the gift inside the cabinet or desk drawer of my office when I wasn't looking.

The one thing that was difficult to tolerate was the language and incidents in the hall that was near my office. The men would swear at each other a lot, and sometimes a brawl would break out.

But all in all, it was a wonderful experience. I remember the mail boat would pull into dock with the mail, and church services would be conducted in the hall.

I remember once when a ship's crew was on strike. The ship was sailing from its origin in upper Michigan, and had docked in Detroit. Because they were in a work protest, the seamen had come ashore. However, they did not have a place to stay, nor any clothes with them. So I helped them find hotel rooms, and took them shopping for some clothes. I also directed them to places where they could eat. This was an interesting situation for them, for they had never dealt with African Americans before, and here they had me taking care of them, almost like a mother, to become acquainted with and settled in the city. They really had no option, other than wandering out on their own. But for seven weeks, these seamen and their strike continued, keeping the ship docked, until the dispute was resolved. This was further demonstration to me of the power of the union, and the reason for the utilization of that power to fight against an unreasonable employer.

It was through an unexpected incident with friends I made through this position that caused me to become engaged in a battle against injustice. One of the top officers, Allen Barahol, was going to get married to a girl that I knew. She was a petite French girl. Allen was the son of a Rabbi, so there was a bit of controversy about this mixed marriage. I had become a friend of both of them as they dealt with this issue. Allen was also dealing with the conflict within his family because he had no interest in becoming a rabbi like his father. But I listened and helped them through this, and even went with them to the City County Building to get their marriage license.

The wedding took place, and the reception dinner was to be held at the restaurant in the Barlum Hotel, which was across the street from the National Maritime Union office. As we all walked in, the management of the restaurant

82

confronted us. They told the group that they would be served, however, they pointed to me and said that they would not serve me. Furthermore, they said that I was not allowed in the restaurant. This not only offended me, but the entire wedding party. As all this transpired, I could see the African American cooks and staff looking through the windows of the kitchen door at the scene. After some words were exchanged, the man who had made the arrangements with the restaurant decided we were all going to walk out, leaving them with a prepared meal, and they refused to pay for it.

Afterwards, I decided that I would not stand for this kind of treatment. By that time, Charles Diggs, Sr., one of the state's first African American senators, and his Polish counterpart, Stanley Nowak, had written into state law a statute that barred discrimination in public places. So the following day, I went to the prosecutor's office. I told the prosecutor what had happened, reminded him of this new law, and told him that every time I was discriminated against, I would report it to him. He supported me, and saw me every time I came in to report something. However, he never did anything to follow up on my complaints.

So I decided to organize a picket line around the Barlum Hotel. It started small, but eventually grew. When the seamen found out what I was doing, and why, they helped. After they'd eat in the union building, they would join the picket line. We continued relentlessly, even during torrential rains. The picket finally ended seven weeks later, when the hotel finally gave in. They decided to end their discriminatory practice, especially after Jack Lawrence, the head of the National Maritime Union, flew in from New York to join the protest.

But another victory against injustice was scored. It was a victory that helped open Detroit restaurants to all people.

CHAPTER FIVE
Progressive Politics & Paul Robeson

After the Barlum Hotel victory, word got around about my ability and desire to break down discrimination. Shortly after the victory, a group of women at the University of Michigan contacted me. On the University's campus, there was a door leading into one of the schools that no woman could enter. I did not know these women, nor do I recall exactly why women were prohibited entrance. But I made the trip out to Ann Arbor to find out what was going on. After explaining the situation to me, they led me to this discriminatory door, and I approached it, opened it, and walked through. Until that very moment, women were prohibited to do so. This incident put my picture on the front page of the Detroit Free Press for the very first time.

*****

The 1948 presidential election was approaching. On April 12, 1945, President Roosevelt had passed, having suffered a cerebral hemorrhage. This put Harry Truman in the White House, and he was seeking re-election as a Democrat. The Republican candidate was Thomas Dewey, who was defeated in the previous presidential race to the highly popular Roosevelt. Dewey had made a positive name for himself as a prosecutor in New York against organized crime, and his years as the governor of New York. The Democrats, however, were hurting due to dissention caused by two factions within the party. The staunch Democrats in the Southern states created their own party known as the States' Rights Party, and backed Strom Thurmond as their presidential candidate, to promote more conservative and prejudicial policies. Supporters of the more liberal policies of the Roosevelt era, including the union movement, backed former vice-president Henry Wallace, as the Progressive Party candidate. Wallace was Roosevelt's vice president during his third term in office (1940-44), but had fallen in disfavor with the Democratic Party. Truman had replaced Wallace as Vice President, and as Secretary of Commerce, Wallace criticized Truman's policies as the interim President. With this unrest within the Democratic Party, Dewey was a favorite to win the presidency.

Wallace spoke out against racial segregation and the discrimination of women, which caught my attention. Furthermore, he sought peace discussions with the USSR, and criticized the stock piling of atomic bombs. He even sought an end to the House Committee on Un-American Activities, which would later become the tool by which Senator Joe McCarthy executed his grand inquisition of Americans.

I was elected to be the National Committee Woman for the State of Michigan for the Progressive Party. A man and a woman were elected to represent each state in the union, and among the Michigan progressives, I was somehow nominated and elected. The person elected as the National Committee Man for the State of Michigan was Coleman Young.

Coleman didn't participate much with the party. I, on the other hand, was more active. I attended a committee meeting in New York, which was an interesting experience. It exposed me to the national aspect of the party, and put me in the same room with some notable people.

I arrived a little early to the hall where the meeting was to be held. Uncertain as to where I was supposed to go, there was what appeared to be an old man, sitting in the hallway. I approached him and asked him if he knew where the meeting room was for the Progressive Party. He raised his head to look at me, his long, wavy, uncombed hair moved away from his face. He informed me that the meeting room was just around the corner, and that he would soon join me. Realizing that he, too, was involved with the party, I introduced myself. I asked him if he was a member of the committee, and he answered that he was. Then he introduced himself as Albert Einstein.

Preventing myself from fainting, I came out of the cloud from having met such an awe-inspiring individual, and walked into the meeting room ahead of him. For a little while, only he and I were sitting in the quiet space of the room. I was so thrilled to be there, but at the same time, tongue-tied. What does one say to someone such as Albert Einstein?

Though we worked hard for Wallace's campaign, the party failed because its leader failed. The conflicts beginning to rise in Korea caused dissention, which brought the party down.

The 1948 election saw the upset of Truman over Dewey. Truman took 49.51% of the popular vote, and 303 Electoral College votes, to Dewey's 45.12% of the popular vote and 189 electoral votes. The States' Rights Party's Strom Thurmond, took 2.4% of the vote and captured 39 electoral votes (South Carolina, Mississippi, Louisiana and Alabama). Wallace received 12,000 popular votes less that Thurmond, achieving 2.38% of the vote, but no electoral votes.

*****

After all the campaigning, the union activities, the challenges to discrimination, and work, I left my job at the National Maritime Union to take a much needed break. After a couple weeks off, I applied for a job at L. B. Arwin and Company. The company was an investment firm. The building the company was located in was on Fort Street, near where the City's main post office is today, and was a docking point for ships. I applied for a secretarial position, and the owner, Lester B. Arwin, was enthused about hiring me, though the "and Company" personnel was not. This was not the first business owned by a white male, with a white staff that I had worked for, nor was there a union to join. In fact, I was replacing the only other African American ever to be hired in the building. But I could utilize my skills there, and earn a decent paycheck, as I returned from my break.

I met a woman named Jeanie, who was the elevator operator. She was French. I had learned to speak some French back in high school, and recalled some of it to communicate with her. She spoke both English and French, but it was fun saying what I could in French, and she taught me more. We became good friends, and she would tell me the gossip of the businesses and warned me of what I could expect being the only African American in the building. Over time, though, I made friends with a number of the secretaries in the building, and we would swap books to read. I would give them a book by Langston Hughes, and they'd respond with a book by Walt Whitman.

My duties included secretarial and clerical responsibilities. I would also run errands for him, like going to the bank. Sometimes, he would send me late in the day. I would have to take the bus to the bank, and by the time I arrived, the bank had closed. However, when the bank employees saw me, they would open the door and allow whatever business Mr. Arwin had sent me there to do. This was a completely new experience for me.

Another duty that came after I had been working there was to assist Mr. Arwin's friends, the Sterbers. The Sterbers were psychiatrists, and Mr. Sterber had suffered an injury resulting from an accident. On Mr. Arwin's behalf, I did whatever they needed, like pay bills and send out letters. As he recuperated, we kept in touch, and I would help him out on occasion. As a gift for my help, the Sterbers gave me this beautiful wool scarf that I'll never forget. Eventually they asked me if I would come over in the evenings to do some work for them. I would take dictation and would type up the casework on people who were receiving help from the Sterbers. I thought I was there to gain more experience and sharpen my secretarial skills. However, through this part-time position, I gained insight into the human condition. When I typed an individual's case history, I would obviously have to read it. In reading these stories and understanding the work of the psychiatrist, I learned that healing involved dealing with a person's whole life. By going back through a person's history, you could find the source of pain and suffering that required attention and healing.

It wasn't long after I began working for Mr. Arwin that I had heard that he had been insulted and threatened to be kicked out of the building for hiring me. I felt extremely bad about this. I talked to him about my concerns and about not wanting him to lose his office because of me. He convinced me that he, as a Jewish man, was willing to take this kind of abuse, and that I should, too. He explained that the only way to break down the barriers of prejudice were to endure such comments and threats, and to show, by example, our quality and equality.

Mr. Arwin subscribed to the Wall Street Journal, and I would read it to learn more about the business world. One morning, I had read an article about the potential growth in the industry of limestone quarrying. Limestone was becoming more prevalent in the production of concrete, and more roads were being built around the nation, which would require more concrete. I mentioned this article to Mr. Arwin in a matter-of-fact manner. He became intrigued with the idea and followed up on it. He took a trip to some location in the American Southwest, and explored the industry and process first hand. Satisfied in what he learned, Mr. Arwin sought to buy into a company called McKirton Limestone Company.

Businessmen from the limestone company would then come to Mr. Arwin's office to negotiate the transaction. They would come in, dressed in their finest suits and stern, cool exteriors, and find me sitting behind the desk in the front office. Their expressions of surprise and their re-examination of the address of the office spoke volumes. But I confirmed that they were at the L. B. Arwin and Company office, and I offered them a place to sit while I notified Mr. Arwin of their presence. Over time, they became used to Mr. Arwin's African American secretary, and in fact, became friendlier with me by conversing with me briefly when they called to speak to Mr. Arwin. Prejudice and discrimination, I have found, can be broken down in many different ways. Sometimes just outright friendliness and humane treatment can dispel the myths within the prejudicial mind.

But in the process, Mr. Arwin became a victim to the practice of discrimination. He could not purchase McKirton Limestone Company on his own, and sought investors and government loans or grants. I wrote a number of the proposals. Unfortunately, he could not gather enough money to make the purchase. He discovered, from reluctant investors, that the cement industry was a very closed market with few suppliers of raw materials. It sought to block any new player into the field, especially a company that was owned by a Jewish man. Furthermore, Lester's wife, Kitty, was a woman of Native American heritage. The cement industry used this as discrimination against Mr. Arwin as well. He eventually gave up on the investment.

Mr. Arwin had also become aware that I openly fought for people's rights and against discrimination, which made Mr. Arwin pretty nervous. Even though he was Jewish, and recognized the need to fight for equal opportunity, Mr. Arwin was a bit conservative and was concerned that my activity would somehow reflect on him and his company. But he wouldn't forbid me from participating. I knew the tension was there, but when I asked Mr. Arwin to leave early from work one day, because there was going to be a parade for the entertainer, Paul Robeson, he agreed to let me leave early to attend. Then, as a participant in the parade, I saw him in the audience. He waved to me as I went by.

*****

Paul Robeson was a controversial figure at the time. As an actor, his stage appearances included Simon the Cyrenian in 1921, All God's Chillun Got Wings in 1924, Show Boat, the musical in 1928, and Othello in 1930 and 1943. My mother and I had seen him perform Othello in Detroit, and his presence and talent astounded my mother. Robeson also appeared in the films Body and Soul in 1924, The Emperor Jones in 1933, Sanders of the River in 1935, and Show Boat in 1936. He also sang, performing often with his friend and collaborator, Lawrence Brown, and releasing record albums. His rendition of Ol' Man River, was, and still is, famous worldwide. Paul Robeson was a gifted entertainer who I had enjoyed watching and listening to.

But entertainment was not his only gift. Robeson was an intelligent man, having graduated from Rutgers in 1919 as valedictorian, took first place in the school's oratorical contest in all four years, and had earned 15 varsity letters in four sports - baseball, football, basketball, and track. He then attended Columbia University Law School, and was admitted to the Bar of New York in 1923. It was while he was in law school that he began acting and met Lawrence Brown. Upon graduation, he obtained a position with Stotesbury and Milner, a New York law firm. However, when a white secretary refused to take dictation from him because he was African American, Robeson left the practice of law to pursue a career on the stage.

Robeson became an international star, as he toured the globe to sing and act. This also allowed him to see more of the world, and the way in which African Americans were treated in other countries in comparison to the United States. Paul was the son of a minister who espoused human rights, of which Paul also spoke about. His graduation speech at Rutgers was titled "The New Idealism," in which he spoke about the fight for the ideal government where one's character would be the standard of excellence, and where black and white hands would clasp in friendship and knowledge that we are all one family of which God is the father.

As World War II had ended, Paul continued to speak for the rights of all people, for unionism, and for an end to the Cold War with the Soviet Union. In 1947, the House Committee on Un-American Activities listed Paul as one of among 1,000 Communists in America. He supported the Henry Wallace campaign for President, but declined the offer to run as Wallace's vice president. As he continued to speak about these issues, his popularity began to fall. Concerts that had been booked were either cancelled or met with violence. On August 27, 1949, a concert of his in Peekskill, New York was stopped due to a riot. The stage was smashed, chairs were torched, and twelve people were sent to the hospital. Robeson vowed to return and eight days later, on September 4th, the concert was held with trade unionists providing security. However, at the concert's conclusion, more chaos erupted, and rioters injured 150 people.

I was participating in the parade, coordinated by the Detroit Committee to Welcome Robeson, which ushered Paul into the City in October, a month after the Peekskill incidents. Afterwards, there was a meeting at Reverend Charles Hill's church - Hartford Avenue Baptist Church. Due to Paul being labeled a Communist, and resistance to allow him to perform on stage, hotel managers were concerned about potential riots and damage if they allowed Robeson to stay at their hotel. Therefore, he did not have a place to stay while in town. Since I lived in a quiet neighborhood, someone asked me if I was willing to allow him to stay in my home. Honored and thrilled at the idea, I did inform them that I lived in a small house, but if he wanted to, my house was welcome to him. They accepted, and I went straight home to tell my mother.

My mother and I immediately had to figure out how to house him. The bedroom was small, and the bed even smaller, especially for his six-foot-two-inch frame. So we took some folding chairs and placed them at the end of the bed, and placed pillows on them, so that he would be able to extend his legs and keep his feet from hitting the floor.

Then, they escorted Paul into the house. Not only did he have the presence of a large, strong man, but also the charisma of a powerful and likeable person. He did not come to the house alone. A caravan of men given the detail to act as bodyguards for him, also stayed while he resided in my home. Among them was Coleman Young.

Paul stayed for about two weeks. I continued to go to work every day, and attended events that Paul participated in. Some days I'd come home, and be amazed to see him outside playing football and other games with the children of the neighborhood. I was initially afraid that something might happen to him, but nothing ever did. The neighborhood was committed to protecting him.

In the evenings when he wasn't out speaking, he would tell us stories about other nations and places he had visited. He told us about places like Vienna, Prague, Budapest, Oslo, Copenhagen, and Stockholm, where he had sung. Places like the Soviet Union, where there was no discrimination. Places like Egypt, where he filmed the movie, Jericho. He told us how people lived in these different places, and was an example to us of how to love all people, regardless of race, color, or creed.

Originally, he was supposed to sing at Sunnie Wilson's Forest Club. However, Sunnie had become reluctant to have Paul on stage. The police department threatened to take his liquor license away, which would have crippled his business. We met with Sunnie at the Gotham Hotel, pleading him not to cancel. He apologized, but said he really had no choice.

So we chose to have Paul sing and speak in the public area known as Grand Circus Park. This would be free and open to anyone and everyone who wanted to hear Paul.

But Sunnie had a conversation with Police Commissioner Harry S. Toy, and talked him into allowing the performance to take place at the Forest Club. The concern was, with Paul singing out in the open, and the embers of the 1943 riots still an underlying tension in the City, and trouble could erupt once more. Wilson convinced Toy that if held at the Forest Club, greater security could be insured, and the crowds contained.

On October 9, 1949, Paul performed before a crowd of 1,800 that packed the Forest Club. Another 1,700 remained outside, unable to get a seat. Prior to the concert, 1,000 police officers circled the massive building to ensure the peace. And peaceful it was. No violence. No shootings.

The time came when Paul had to move on. And though he left, he would return to Detroit on occasion.

Photographer unknown

PAUL ROBESON WITH ME & ROBERTA BARROW

He was in Detroit in April of 1954. By then, he had been banned from the television. The government demanded his passport as a response to his denouncement of the Korean War. He was shunned by African American leaders, and was blacklisted from performing in halls, auditoriums and churches. His wife, Eslanda, was called before the House Un-American Activities Committee, and had refused to comply with their interrogation. It happened to be his birthday, April 9, 1954, when he turned 56. I decided to celebrate his birthday at my house. I invited two children - Arthur Carter, who was my godchild, and his brother. The children I was raising, my niece and nephew, Patrya and Phillip, and the children of another friend also attended. Coleman Young came along as Paul's bodyguard, and the small party devoured a twenty-one pound roast in no time flat. The children were well behaved. It was a treat, but also dangerous, for this was during the McCarthy era, as he led the House Un-American Activities Committee on a witch hunt for Communists, destroying the professional lives of so many people, including Paul Robeson's. Any one who spoke out against the government's actions or policies was subject to being labeled a Communist. I know that my activities, particularly my support of Paul Robeson and activity in unionism, brought me under surveillance by the FBI. Coleman Young had been called before the House Un-American Activities Committee two years prior, but for whatever reason, I was not.

And still, I treasured the friendship that I had made with Paul and Eslanda. I learned a great deal from his tales of travel that it inspired me to travel the world. I remained friends whenever I saw them while touring the country. Eslanda died of cancer in 1965, and Paul died of two strokes within a month's time, in 1976. Two years prior, in 1974, the FBI finally ended its investigation of Paul Robeson.

*****

In 1952, I had achieved as high a position as I could at L. B. Arwin and Company, so I decided that it was time to leave. I had discovered an opportunity to go into business for myself, and decided to take it.

The business was selling furnaces and air conditioning units to buildings. Not directly, obviously, for I had no space to store them. I was a sales representative, and opened up an office on the second floor of a building, above a nightclub, at John R. and Milwaukee, a block from Grand Boulevard. My company came to be known as Arden Enterprises.

The reason I went into this particular business was because I knew a lot of churches and the people who were in charge of them. Unfortunately, my percentage of the sale was rather low.

One of my supporters was Mother Bracy of Church of God in Christ. She was a wonderful woman who taught me much more about the healing community and the necessity of working together. The church and its parishioners became my customers.

Mother Bracy approached me about selling a product of her own. Bath salts. She had purchased a bath salts company in Highland Park and took me out to the facility to show me. It was a warehouse, more or less, with mountains of bath salts all over. Mother Bracy wanted to fill individual packages so that she could sell them to people. So I helped her in this venture.

Mother Bracy had no skills in business. She was in the health care field. So I contacted Lester Arwin and asked if he would help Mother Bracy with marketing her product, which he did. Then, I began selling the bath salts for her, and she was beginning to make a little money from this. It was enough money that it was becoming unsafe for her to carry it around in her purse. So I took her down to the Bank of the Commonwealth, and showed her how to open a bank account. Once that was established, I would take the money from the bath salts sales I had made and deposited into her account.

Through this experience, I learned more about marketing and operating one's own business that I ever imagined existed. Through Mother Bracy, I was again engaged in the community, in that she would encourage me to adopt children from her church to help educate them on the kinds of things people need to do, like open bank accounts and operate a business. She made sure I got to conventions and set me up to speak at the women's meetings they held at the church. At that time, I thought I had done everything I could do, but Mother Bracy taught me that there was so much more to do to help the community. This returned my thoughts to going back to school to get a degree in social work.

One of my most thrilling moments came when I was allowed to sit next to Bishop Mason at one of the annual women's meetings at the church. Bishop Mason had founded Church of God in Christ, and at the time, was 90 years old.

I was in awe of him. His skin smooth like a baby's, and he was so strong and luminous when he spoke at the platform.

I moved my office to 275 East Ferry Street, in Ferry Center, a lovely two-story mansion. This was also the home office for Maxine Powell's Finishing School, Detroit's first African American-owned modeling business. Maxine Powell owned and operated the school, as well as the building.

I remember my first meeting with her. I walked into the building to discuss with her about the possibility of renting office space. I waited on Miss Powell to come from wherever she was. She called out from another room to let me know that she would be with me in a minute. After a few minutes, this big door opened, and this little lady came walking through, all dressed up in sooty clothes. I told the lady that I was waiting for Miss Powell, and she said, "I'm Miss Powell." Confused, I asked her what was happening, and she said, "Oh, I was just downstairs fixing the furnace." This was my first exposure to the polished teacher of etiquette and modeling.

Maxine grew up in Chicago, and had graduated from the John Robert Powers School, a charm instruction and modeling school. After a visit to Detroit in the 1940's, she decided to move here in 1948. Two years later, she opened her Finishing School. It was not only a school to teach men and women etiquette and modeling, but she also hosted wedding receptions, dances, and fashion shows. And if you wanted to know about anything socially going on in Detroit, she knew it all. Eventually, she was a major influence on the Motown stars, when Berry Gordy's sister, Gwen, convinced him that Maxine had something to teach their future stars. She polished many Motown greats, such as Smokey Robinson, Martha and the Vandellas, Diana Ross and the Supremes, Stevie Wonder, and the Temptations.

I chipped in and helped her out, not as a paid employee, but as a person who wanted to learn about this profession. I helped with her advertising and promotional work.

I had also become involved with Bertha Gordy, Berry's wife, and the Gordy family. Bertha had become a member of the Lady Camille Temple.

This was my connection to Motown, one of the most important and artistically influential contributions Detroit gave to America.

I operated Arden Company and helped Maxine Powell for as long as I could, but the message was becoming clear to me from my pocketbook. I didn't have the finances to pay for the furnaces and have them installed, and take on the debt of the customers. Even with Reverend Dr. Ann Ryan and Onslow Parrish helping me as members on the board of directors of my company, I was not going to be able to make a living at this, and I had to move on.

CHAPTER SIX
Elks & Donkeys

As I mentioned earlier, I had established the Lady Camille Temple No. 755 in April of 1943. However, my involvement with the Elks lasted many years beyond that.

The Benevolent Protective Order of the Elks (BPOE) had been a predominantly white organization, and had resisted the advancement of African Americans. In the early months of 1898, B.F. Howard and Arthur J. Riggs established an African American Elks organization in Cincinnati, Ohio. This created friction, and the organization was under constant harassment, as was its leaders. In fact, Riggs moved his family to Springfield, Ohio, and changed his name because he was blacklisted from obtaining a job in Cincinnati. By the end of 1899, the Improved Benevolent Protective Order of the Elks of the World (IBPOE of W) was established. Relations remained bad between the IBPOE of W and the BPOE, with the latter challenging the former over the trademark of rituals, the logo, and in name. Finally, in 1918, the BPOE officially ended its opposition to the IBPOE of W.

About a year after my temple was established, the director of public relations asked me if I would serve as the Directress of Public Relations for the women of the Elks. I agreed, and served with Charles P. McLean of Sealton, Pennsylvania. Each year, we would meet and work out the public relations program for the year.

I had traveled to Atlanta, Georgia for the IBPOE of W Convention. It was held at Main Street Baptist Church. The convention halls would not rent their space to African Americans, and hotels would not accommodate African Americans with a room. The friends and families of members of IBPOE of W hosted those of us who traveled to Atlanta. I remember going out with some of the ladies to do some shopping one afternoon. Inside one of the department stores, I became thirsty and sought out a drinking fountain. There were two fountains, with a sign above each. One read, "Whites," the other read "Colored." I got over my thirst real quick, and walked out. I was determined not to shop in these kinds of stores, and I certainly would not purchase or recommend others to purchase from these stores. I did not want to support such businesses that chose to discriminate against African Americans.

In 1952, I remember the week-long convention we held in Atlantic City, New Jersey. We were sponsoring programs of education and development for our youth to become leaders in the community. We were only given a small school to use to present our material. So I called the press to have them get the word out and cover our event. I told them that 75,000 people would be involved. But the media ignored us. They challenged my claim that 75,000 people would be in attendance.

On Tuesday of that week, we held our parade. The attendance was estimated to be 75,000 people. We received media coverage that day. It was later discovered that more money had been deposited by businesses in the banks of Atlantic City that day than on any day previous, due to the mass of people we drew, who spent money in the city. Imagine how many more people would have been involved had we been allowed to take our parade down the Boardwalk. We were prohibited from that location. But the parade through the African American neighborhoods was effective.

Martin Luther King Jr. spoke at our 1955 convention. It was a powerful speech. He had won our national oratorical competition when he was younger, which provided a scholarship for him to attend college. He was so appreciative of the financial help the Elks provided. I was especially proud of him. Here I was, approaching 40 years old, having fought against discrimination with the intent of not destroying any person, or getting even with anyone, but rather, fighting to eliminate the mindset through the power of Divine Love. And here was this young, 25 year-old man, pursuing the same dream with the same approach. And shortly thereafter, on December 1, 1955, Rosa Parks was arrested for refusing to give up her seat to a white male, on a Montgomery, Alabama bus.

The international scope of the Elks fostered my desire to participate in worldwide affairs, to help settle the problems of the world and achieve peace and unity. I wanted to know more about the African people all around the world, for in every land, in every country, there was a community of African people included within their population. The Elks also fostered the historical recognition of white Americans who fought against slavery in the United States. For example, the organization owned a piece of property known as Harper's Ferry in Virginia, which was the former home of John Brown. I had the opportunity to visit the historical landmark, and experience the people's poverty of that area of the country. The poverty of the hills as they called it, was where whole families were living with next to nothing, financially.

The Elks allowed me to travel often, and as I continue through my story, I may speak to more of the travels as they relate to my life. For now, let me close my story on my involvement with the Elks by saying that I had served as the Grand Directress of Public Relations for thirty years, which included years I was on the Detroit City Council. Upon the conclusion of my tenure, the IBPOE of W bestowed upon me their highest honor. The Elijah P. Lovejoy Award. Named after the white American printer from Detroit who used his printing press to help fight for the end of slavery as a part of the abolition movement, it is an honor awarded to someone of importance to the African American story. It is a high honor for me to have been recognized with this award.

*****

After Henry Wallace's loss in the 1948 election, I still felt a need to continue being active in helping get good candidates elected to office. I was intrigued to learn that an African American woman was running for a state senate position. Her name was Cora Mae Brown. So I volunteered to help in her campaign, and in 1952, she won, becoming the first African American woman to be elected as a state senator. However, she served her full term, then disappeared, never to be heard from again in the political world.

Stanley Nowak was my introduction to the Polish community. Through my work with him and his wife Margaret, the community adopted me into its family. I encountered no prejudice, discrimination or evil. In fact, there was a woman who gave me the key to the house that was the campaign office for Stanley Nowak. I could go in the back door and use a bedroom if I needed a place to rest, or use the office to help campaign. The woman who owned the house would often cook for us. I can still smell the sauerkraut. It seems like we had sauerkraut for breakfast, lunch, and dinner.

Food is a common language, yet unique to all our different cultures. A wonderful way to share in another's culture is to share a meal with them.

Stanley Nowak and his wife Margaret and I became dear friends. He was a good man, with the community's interests at heart. I worked very hard for him to become elected to the Detroit City Council, which he did not achieve. He had combined forces with Charles Diggs Sr., as they ran together as a black-white team that was a benefit to the City of Detroit and State of Michigan. Prior to running for City Council, while serving in the Michigan senate, they co-authored a bill to eliminate discrimination in restaurants and other public places, which passed through the State legislature and became law.

During the campaign, I remember a particular incident. One young man who was assisting the campaign by distributing flyers promoting the Diggs-Nowak team, was hauled down to the police station while distributing them at Eastern Market. It was my responsibility to go and rescue him. Outside of my exposure of brutality inflicted by the police department during the 1943 riot, I was naive to the operation of a police station.

So I went down to the 7th Precinct, which was then located on Gratiot and St. Aubin. I was amazed at what I encountered. The police commander sat in this high desk, so high that you had to look up at them. Subconsciously, a person was under the authoritative rule of the police commander. After the initial shock, I pleaded the case of the boy whom they had picked up. The commander, and other police officers, looked at me as if I was crazy, partially because I was not intimidated by the lofty perch of judgment that he sat upon, but also because I was an African American woman fighting on behalf of a white male. They questioned me about my identity, and I informed them that I was in charge of Stanley Nowak's campaign. I testified to the boy's innocence in passing out campaign literature (they had picked him up for some other misdeed), that he was doing as instructed under my authority, and that he was of good moral character.

A couple of the police officers held a discussion about the situation, and finally released the boy. Maybe because they were amazed to see an African American woman act so foolish in front of them, or maybe because they didn't have enough reason to hold him. I was relieved just to get him out of there. The whole incident felt like I was dealing with the Gestapo.

*****

Elvin Davenport asked me to help him run for Judge. I accepted. He won his election with relative ease, and though I did not have a lot to do with his campaign, it provided me with the strength and self-assurance to join the campaign team for Bill Patrick.

Bill Patrick was a lawyer, and he was running for City Council in 1957. There had been no African American in a City Council position since the 1800's when an African American alderman had been elected. I worked with his campaign manager, but was not impressed with the way in which he applied himself. The campaign manager was more interested in entertaining people. I took charge and helped direct the campaign. I utilized the Twelve Horsemen Civic Center as the campaign headquarters, and enlisted the help of a lot of people. We were able to get Patrick into a number of churches to speak, even into churches that had never had a politician appear before the congregation, and Bill spoke to them. When the votes were finally counted, the City of Detroit, and the African American community, had a representative on the City Council.

I was filled with joy at having been a part of his campaign victory. But it was equally disappointing to me when he left City Council before the end of his term, to accept a better job in New York. His victory had the desired impact, as the door was now open for African Americans to become elected to City Council. Reverend Nicholas Hood Jr., an outstandingly known and graciously kind person, was next to be elected. Ernie Brown and Robert Tindal followed.

Throughout all this campaigning, I found myself immersed amongst the many cultures within the City of Detroit. This was a wonderful experience for me; however, it placed a question mark over me in the eyes of some people in the African American community. Some questioned whom it was I was really representing.

They didn't understand that the big picture I was seeking to achieve was to open the door of political office to the African American community, and in particular, within the City of Detroit. It was about breaking down the barriers of prejudicial thought and separation amongst people by the color of their skin. It was about showing other citizens of Detroit that there were African American citizens who were competent leaders, concerned for all of Detroit's citizens. To achieve that, I was a diplomat between the cultures, helping foster peace within our city, and develop love and understanding with each other. My vision was of unity and strength amongst the people of Detroit. Detroit is one people, with many voices and backgrounds.

Success was made at getting African Americans elected. And though I sought to continue building on this success, my personal life required attention.

CHAPTER SEVEN
Change

The period of the 1950's and early into the 1960's were personally challenging times. Yes, I did keep myself busy. I was working as a trainer for Fuller Products on Broadway Street. Fuller Products was a company started by Mr. S. B. Fuller, a wealthy African American from Chicago. His business was the door-to-door sales of cosmetics. My job was to train the sales people. I would arrive at work early in the morning, prepare and research the products, then train sales people on the Fuller product line. The book that was provided by the company to use in its training instruction was Napoleon Hill's "Think and Grow Rich." Also, I was involved with the Elks, and managing campaigns for politicians. But this became a time of change in my personal life.

My mother was suffering from ulcers, and my Aunt Maude was also at an advanced age. Patrya and Philip, the daughter and son of my sister Doris, were also growing up and living with me, in a house I had purchased on French Road. In order to settle a difficulty with her husband, Doris left Patrya and Philip in my care. These issues and financial issues were very stressful on me.

In addition, I had to travel to Pensacola, Florida, to bring my Aunt Harriet to my home, in order to avoid having her put in a nursing home. This was a traumatic move for her. She had never left Pensacola. She resisted all the way. I was able to bring most of her furnishings, and once we moved her in, she became a member of the family. However, she only seemed to accept me, which created some friction with everyone else. But she was a very able woman, at 89 years old, and eventually made friends with the neighbors.

I was involved with Reverend Dr. Ann Ryan's church, the Divine Temple of Mental Science, and would take my mother, aunts (including Aunt Harriet who loved to attend), and children to her church.

But in 1958, my mother passed away.

I have spoken a lot, throughout this story, about how much my mother meant to me. She was supportive of every cause I stood for, and of every battle I fought. She was an intelligent and strong woman, having to raise both me and my sister. I mentioned the work she did at Michigan Mutual Liability Hospital. They had fired her because she had developed both a tumor and goiter. She eventually was compensated with thirteen weeks of pay. Due to Reverend Ryan's metaphysical treatments, the tumor and goiter eventually disappeared.

Back when I was working at Great Lakes Mutual Insurance, with the Mahoneys, factories were hiring women for positions as the men were off to war. My mother sought one of those positions, and both she and I picked up the pre-employment test. This test was for a supervisory position, and on the test was this extremely difficult math problem. I tried to work it, but no matter how hard I tried, I just could not figure out the answer to that problem. My mother, however, with her eighth grade education, solved it. This was just another demonstration to me that growing up in a period where education was not easily accessible to African Americans, especially in the south, my mother and my family, achieved great knowledge and skills despite the conditions. We learned that she solved the problem, and she was awarded the job at the factory. But she had to decline the position. My grandfather in Alabama had died, and she needed to go there to help with the arrangements. The job was something special, an opportunity that would come ever so rarely, especially in those days to an African American woman. But her heart was with her family, and that was most important to her. The loss of my mother weighed heavily on me.

*****

I mentioned the children - Patrya and Philip. Patrya was born in 1942, and Phillip in 1943, to my sister, Doris. At some point in the late 1940's, early 1950's, when the children were around eight or nine years old, my sister was living a rather hard life, and was having challenges with her husband. In order for her to save herself, and the children, Doris placed them in my care. I had instantly and reluctantly become a parent to my niece and nephew.

I have never given birth to a child, but raising Patrya and Phillip taught me plenty about being a mother. My mother had set a great example of being a mother, and I can only hope and pray that I have been a positive influence on them. My parenting style was not like my mother's, in that, she would go to work and then come home and take care of us. Rather, I was involved in many organizations outside of my job that I relied greatly on my mother and Aunt Maude's help.

Patrya was very smart in school. She was one of those brilliant little girls stuck in a man's world. I remember having to go to battle for her at Southeastern High School. She was, as I said, a very bright child, and she wanted to take a class in drafting. Mind you, this was the late 1950's, in the days when there were distinct lines as to what boys could do and what girls could do. And drafting was one of those vocational classes placed on the side of what boys could do. Patrya wanted to take the class, and was the only girl who was interested in taking the class. The teacher, a man, of course, would not allow her to sign up for it.

Well, I went to the school to talk to this teacher. His concern was that she would be the only girl in the class, which may subject her to problems. I told him that she should be allowed in the class, and if the boys couldn't handle it, that would be their problem. I also reminded him that my tax dollars provided a seat in his class for her. He gave in and Patrya took the class, and ended the year with one of the highest grades. I was so impressed with her achievement, I started searching out how she could get a job in that profession or to go to college and get a degree in that area. However, I ran into discrimination again. Most of the schools Patrya applied to would not let her into the program due to a clause that admitted students of relatives who had attended the school. Today, it is referred to as a legacy admission, or the wealthy person's affirmative action.

I then sought to get her scholarships to schools in the south, and she was accepted by Bennett College in North Carolina. Unfortunately, I was unable to put together enough money to send her. And Patrya had goals of her own. She wanted to take the drafting class, but not necessarily pursue it as a vocation. Instead, her focus was not to further her education out of high school, but rather, wanted to get married. So I prepared a wedding for her. It was a beautiful wedding. Merrill J. Williams, a friend of my family, drove in from Ohio, and helped me with it. She actually made Patrya's wedding dress. It was elegant and stately.

Patrya married, and eventually gave birth to my granddaughter, Anne Francine. Today, both Patrya and Anne are very successful in their lives. Patrya is an expert at holistic living and nutrition. Anne is a designer.

Phillip was a year younger than Patrya. He was a sensitive, fragile soul, unable to withstand the torment of other children on the streets and in school. As a young boy, he became involved in Boy Scouts. However, to do so, I had to buy him a scout uniform and send him to camp. Again, this was an economically challenging time for me, but I was fortunate to have a Hudson's charge account, and was able to charge the uniform. I remember the day I dropped him off and the bus took him and his friends to camp. He was the happiest boy on the planet. However, upon his return, he was sad and despondent. I wondered what was wrong, and he told me. A friend he had made at the camp had drowned. The little boy did not survive. This devastated Phillip, and its effects were felt by me. The child that had lost his life could have easily been Phillip. I consoled him, and discovered a deep sense of appreciation of children. They are so fragile and innocent, yet bursting with the potential for a long life. A person has to enjoy each and every moment she has with a child, because they do not stay children forever. Sometimes fate snatches them from us, and most times, they grow up to adulthood. A child's sense of wonder and self should be appreciated constantly.

Philip grew up and joined the army. Then, he became involved in the community, under the guiding wing of Chris Austin. When the Forest Park area of the city had been declared uninhabitable, Chris Austin and his wife, Marti, went to City Hall, and fought for the opportunity to turn the area into something respectable. They set up an office in an abandoned home. Chris, Marti, and Carolyn Taylor, created a print shop, which started the process. A variety of projects emerged, such as the Black Research Foundation, whose goal was to research, investigate, and write about African American history. Phillip, Patrya, and I contributed our time to helping in any way that we could. Phillip became very involved. Chris had become a mentor to Phillip, and Phillip worked diligently to help Chris and their development of Forest Park. Currently, apartment buildings and a community center exist at Forest Park, which would not have were it not for Chris' efforts.

Phillip died of AIDS in the 1990's. He moved in with me as the disease took over his body. I had to keep the house immaculately clean and sanitized. I took care of him until he finally had to be admitted into a hospital. He left behind a beautiful daughter named Charita, who had an excellent singing voice. She now has a daughter named Corsica, who we all have high hopes for to be a star. She is eight years old, and has a beautiful singing voice. She was able to spend her early years of school at the Erma Henderson Institute of International Studies, Commerce, and Technology.

*****

During this time, we were living in my house on French Road. I loved that house. I lived next to a Frenchman who was an engineer. He helped Patrya develop her talents and interest in that drafting class I spoke of earlier. It was the house Paul Robeson stayed in back in 1949, for those two weeks that we were trying to get Sunnie Wilson to have him perform and speak at the Forest Club, and, a few years later, when we held his birthday party there. There was a backyard where the children could play and plant gardens. Though a lot of turbulence was going on in my life at that point, the house provided a solid ground where I felt secure.

However, I was beginning to spend a lot of money updating and fixing the house. And with mother gone, Patrya married, and Phillip in the army, there was no reason for me to stay in the house alone. I decided it was time to sell, and move on.

*****

As you recall, when I was younger, I wondered about the experience of God. I didn't feel anything unusual when I prayed. I only felt the cold water of my baptism. What did it mean to hear God speak, or have an experience of God?

Since that time, and up to this point in the late 1950's, early 1960's, I had God experiences. The communication was never a direct voice talking to me, but rather, just a knowing that God was communicating and guiding me. However, because of the stress and changes my life was going through at this time, I had my first experience of God's communication through a thundering voice.

To relieve the stress I was experiencing I started smoking. It did not become a daily habit. However, instead of seeking inner peace through meditation or other healthy ways, I would smoke a cigarette. By this time, I was in my mid-forties, and not having been well practiced at smoking, I began to develop a regular cough. It wasn't that noticeable, unless I was lying down. So while I tried to sleep, I'd cough throughout the night. To relieve me of this, someone had suggested that I drink a little brandy to help me sleep. But I decided not to try that remedy.

One night, I was in bed, trying to sleep, but coughing instead. Then, I heard it. It wasn't audible to the human ear. It echoed throughout every cell of my being. A thunderous, booming voice spoke to me.

"Erma, look at what you're doing to my chest," God said. I saw myself laying there, as if I were standing next to the bed, looking down on myself, and all of a sudden, I could see my chest being opened. It was filled with smoke. "I have walked through life with you to keep you clean, and look at what you're doing to muddy up your body." I knew I had two packs of cigarettes on the nightstand, "God, I'm throwing those away, and I'll never buy or borrow another cigarette."

The experience was so memorable and so powerful. As I tell this story, it still sends chills through me.

*****

Change is inevitable. It is a part of life. It is a part of growth. It is important to recognize it, and adapt to it, in order for your dreams and goals to manifest. Is it sometimes frustrating? Of course it is. I know that my life is God's to direct, even though sometimes God's plan differs from my idea of what the plan should be.

CHAPTER EIGHT
Equal Justice For All

In the early 1960's, I became involved in a project conducted by Michigan Bell Telephone. It was called Assist Negro Youth, and its goal was to improve the relationship between the races and between the citizens and the police department. The Detroit Police Department was a predominantly white police force, whose hostilities toward the non-white citizens of Detroit had not diminished since the riots of the 1940's. Michigan Bell joined with a City authority to insist on having the white police officers participate in this program.

The program was undertaken during the summer, when the children were out of school and consisted of matching a white police officer with an African American child. The officer would take the child out to a ball game, or to the zoo, or something like that. It was a way in which the innocence of a child could touch the heart of a police officer, opening the officer to the realization of the shared humanity between the races. Many officers resisted the program, however by summer's end, they came through for the children and for themselves.

I was very active at the Divine Temple of Mental Science, with Reverend Dr. Ann Ryan. She had achieved the second step of her path by having purchased a building to conduct her spiritual services in, and had broken ground on the third step of the path - the construction of her church. When the construction of the church was completed, Dr. Ryan became the first woman in Detroit to build a church from the ground up. I was inspired by her, and supported her every step of the way. The congregation of her church was a beautiful mix of people. Her practice and teaching of metaphysical principles inspired many, and her services were spiritual and thoughtful, with glorious music.

But with all the campaigning I had done, and the people I met while selling furnaces, I was establishing a connection with many of the churches in Detroit. They all felt like home to me, regardless of denomination. Even the few churches that I had a difference of opinion with regarding their philosophy or practices, I knew that the love of God flowed and presided in the hearts of its congregation. It was one of the many blessings I experienced being involved in the campaigns for various candidates for public office.

*****

The Federal Government created a program known as Model Neighborhoods, whereby certain poverty stricken areas of cities would be identified and the program would then be instituted. Government-like structures would be created within these neighborhoods, managed by the people who lived within the neighborhood, and government funds would be granted to them based on need. In Detroit, the project was known as TAAP, or Total Action Against Poverty. I, with Patrya and Phillip, became active in this project.

Any person, who lived within one of these impoverished areas, could emerge as a leader and spokesperson for the area. Generally, in neighborhoods such as these, the only development of leadership came through the churches. But it was amazing to see the number of people who blossomed and emerged as leaders. People who could hardly read or write. People who could hardly speak intelligently.

118

People who had not graduated high school. People who were advanced in years. It was a great lesson for me to learn about leadership. Leadership has nothing to do with one's formal education, one's wealth, one's race or one's age. There is a leader within each of us, waiting to emerge.

Forest Park was on Forest Street, an area within a few miles of City Hall, and as far back as 1936, it had been declared uninhabitable. The City was always going to set aside funds to rebuild this area within a predominantly Polish neighborhood. Unfortunately, the City only got as far as the "going to" stage. The area was an eyesore for the City, especially being so close to City Hall, and it was an embarrassment that such a dilapidated neighborhood could exist like that, with no hope of improvement, except for tearing it down and rebuilding.

The Sweetest Heart of Mary Catholic Church was at the heart of the neighborhood, and was one of the Catholic church's most beautiful edifices. The church actively participated in TAAP, opening its doors and offering its leadership to the neighborhood. At the other end of Forest Street, at St. Aubin, was another Catholic church which did not participate at all.

Chris Austin, a labor leader in the area, took a pro-active part in building this community. As I mentioned previously, Phillip looked to Chris as a mentor, and Chris helped Phillip mature. In fact, Phillip was able to live in the first apartment house that had been built, at a rent of only $125 per month. Chris was fundamental in laying the groundwork for the development of this area. New developments emerged, which were also citizen-owned and managed under citizen district councils. The Diggs homes, named after the former U.S. Congressman, was a private development that was also a benefit to the area.

However, an ugly rumor surfaced about the developments. I cannot substantiate it, however it was strong enough of a rumor that it caused people to leave these neighborhoods. The rumor was that the government would target those neighborhoods that were designated as Model Neighborhoods, and unleash germs in an effort to learn about new diseases and how to cure them. Again, there is nothing to substantiate this, but it was powerful enough to cause people to become afraid, and they would move out of the neighborhood However, the rumor could not prevent the growth and development of the leaders that emerged from those Model Neighborhoods. Many of those leaders continued to grow and develop, taking on new challenges and rising to greater heights, all the way through the years Coleman Young was mayor.

The man who headed TAAP later became a professor of sociology and social work at Wayne State University. He was instrumental in recognizing the African American individuals within the project who took on leadership positions, and those who required some training, and fought very hard for them. One of the things he was able to achieve was the ability to grant licenses of social work to the leaders of the program. This included Patrya and myself.

*****

As drug use became more prevalent in the City of Detroit, I had been called upon to study the use of methadone as a treatment for drug addiction. This occurred in or around 1967, and I had to learn about the process and present it to City Council. During this process, violent disturbances erupted in Detroit.

The story is familiar to many, because it put Detroit in the national spotlight. On the morning of Sunday, July 23, 1967, white Detroit police officers raided a celebration honoring the return of African American servicemen from Vietnam. This occurred at what was called a "blind pig," which was the label used on establishments that illegally sold alcohol after hours. The police officers threw someone down the stairs of the building, and beat up a few others. Because so many people were there, the police failed to provide enough back-up to transport those they were going to arrest. The police transferred as many as they could, while others were held to wait for the next wave of police cars and vans to arrive. Citizens that lived in the neighborhood, who were not involved in the original incident, got involved, which created the conditions that incited the violence. A brick that was hurled and smashed the back window of one of the police cars was the spark that caused the explosion.

The week to follow saw a mass display of looting, destruction, and fires that turned the city upside down. By the end of the week, 4,400 Detroit police officers, 8,000 National guardsmen, 4,700 federal troops and 360 Michigan state police were patrolling the streets of Detroit. I was among many citizens, like Martha Jean "the Queen" Steinberg and others, who were in the streets during the disturbances, trying to bring peace and help, as armored tanks rolled through. This, as you can imagine, was an extremely dangerous action, however there were many in the community who were willing to put an end to this violence, of which I was one. In fact, I did have a terrifying experience. I was in my home, holding the baby of a friend of mine who was staying with me. I held a baby in my arms and approached the home's front window. As I looked out, a National Guardsman was pointing a rifle directly at me. Fortunately, he did not shoot.

Forty-three people died as a result. Of the 43 killed, 33 were African American, and 10 were white. Furthermore, the 43 deaths breakdown as follows:

18	killed by Detroit police officers
6	killed by National guardsmen
5	killed by Detroit police officers and National guardsmen working together (of which 4 of those killed were innocent of wrongdoing).
2	killed by storeowners
3	killed by private citizens
2	looters died in a fire.
2	killed by downed power lines.
1	Army paratrooper accidentally killed a 19-year-old man.

1	unknown gunman killed a 23-year-old visitor to the city through the window of his hotel.
1	firefighter killed by the bullet of either a sniper or National guardsman.
1	a police officer was killed as a fellow officer struggled with a prisoner.
1	killed at the Algiers Motel (he was present in the room when police officers killed the other two occupants of the room).

Furthermore, 467 people were injured, of which:

-181 were civilians
-167 were Detroit police officers
-83 were Detroit fire fighters
-17 were National Guard
-16 were Michigan state police
-3 U.S. Army service personnel.[1]

As a result of the violence, 7,231 people were arrested. A majority (6,407) were African American, while 824 were white. The youngest person arrested was 10 years old, and the oldest was an 82-year-old white man. Only 3% of those arrested went to trial, and 50% of those were acquitted.

Some have suggested that this was a race riot. But in truth, it had nothing to do with dissention between white residents and African American residents. Rather, it had to do with a militant police department that held its citizens in disregard, particularly African American citizens.

Due to this ugly week in Detroit's history, I became more interested in criminal justice. Attorney Arthur Boman, who originally directed me to study methadone treatment as an aid to recover from drug addiction, called on me to pursue a different course.

---

[1] Statistics from the Detroit Almanac: 300 Years of Life in the Motor City, listed in the Sources section.

*****

Detroit Recorder's Court had developed a reputation because of the judgments coming out of the court. Dr. Donald I. Warren, a sociologist from the University of Michigan, became interested in the issue and sought to conduct a study. An organization called Equal Justice Council was developed to assist in the gathering of information for Dr. Warren's report.

Arthur Boman approached me to ask if I would be interested in working as the director of Equal Justice Council. My duties would begin as an assistant to the current director. His status was temporary because he had to leave the city for personal reasons, and I would then assume the director's position. I accepted.

I was involved in recruiting volunteers to be trained for a week to be court watchers. The training included learning the procedures of the court, how to observe the process, and how to document what was observed for the purpose of the study. After the week's training, the volunteers would then attend court sessions and document their observations.

Volunteers were hard to find, at first, but as word got around, they began to trickle in. One of our early observations about the volunteers was that it was very difficult to find African Americans who would volunteer to be a court watcher. This altered our focus towards the schools of higher education and their students. I spoke with a sociology professor at Marygrove College, who then began directing many student volunteers to our program. This enabled us to have court watchers in every courtroom on any given day.

Recorder's Court was an old building, just behind what has now become Greek Town. On the other side of the street was St. Mary's Catholic Church. Our office was located in a German Catholic church nearby.

The program became well known throughout the community, for we advertised for volunteers at all the religious and social work institutions within the city, drawing in fresh people with ideas. This was an exciting challenge and activity for me to be engaged in.

As we started the court-watching program, the judges would appear at their bench around two o'clock in the afternoon, and leave around five o'clock. Most were visiting judges, not specifically elected to sit on the bench. So they would be coming from other district court houses, hear cases for about an hour or two, then leave. This caused a stressful situation for the rest of the courtroom. People would be scheduled to appear in the morning, spend half the day waiting to be heard, and sometimes would not be heard at all. In addition to that, other situations contributed to the chaos. For example, people were being held in jail for as long as a year as a result of the 1967 disturbances. Miranda warnings were often not given. People were being arrested and thrown in jail at what seemed to be at the whim of the police.

I remember one instance where a judge dismissed forty-seven cases because the defendants had already served one year without ever having come to trial.

Most of the people brought before the court were poor, African American, foreign born, or women. The judges on the bench were predominately white males. It was clear that the people who were disadvantaged received unfair treatment.

The courtroom itself created an obstacle to justice. It was an old building with absolutely no convenience. A person could go and sit there all day without an opportunity to eat. Restroom facilities were inadequate. The lack of air conditioning created a stale, dank, and sometimes heavy air within the building. Also, there wasn't a private location where a person could consult with his or her attorney. The citizen would have to speak with the lawyer outside the courtroom, amidst the rest of the traffic and goings on. And lawyers would have to enter the courtroom, and locate the person he or she would have to represent, during the proceedings of another case.

The jail was old and decrepit, and the people were housed in close quarters to each other. The building had seen many many years of use, however not to the increasing level of activity that was suddenly thrust upon it.

Within the halls of the courthouse was a group of lawyers that were sarcastically referred to as the Clinton Street Bar Association. They had no offices of their own. They merely hung around the courtrooms and bargained with people who would be appearing before the court, in order to represent them. If the person agreed, the lawyer would stand in for him, plead the case, then collect his money and move on in search of his next client.

Equal Justice Council became a major influence. The court watchers were diligent, prompt, and accurate. The Marygrove College students were receiving college credit for their efforts. Other groups chipped in with support, such as the YWCA from the suburbs. Retired persons and housewives volunteered.

As our mission to gather data continued, we took on another project. We fought to obtain a decent building for a new courthouse. We wanted a courthouse where courtrooms would have an adjacent room where the charged and the attorney could meet in private. We wanted courtrooms with a sound system installed and microphones for the judge, the witness, and the attorney, so that everyone could hear each other. We put together our proposal in a professional manner, and eventually got that new courthouse built. Frank Murphy Hall of Justice.

With the new courthouse, the old courthouse was scheduled to be torn down. So Equal Justice Council led a charge to call for a new jail to be built where the old court house once stood. The proposal for a jail was placed on the ballot, and between Equal Justice Council and New Detroit, we were able to get the ballot passed, which called for millions of dollars to build the jail from the county. However, a delay in the construction caused the funds to dwindle. There was resistance within the community to having the jail built. Because of these obstacles, the funds provided were not enough to construct the kind of jail that we had wanted, but nonetheless, a jail was built, which was better than the old jail.

As the new jail was being constructed, the old jail was still in use. So we tried to make the best of it until the day it would be closed. I introduced, through Equal Justice Council, a jail ministry. This began with ministers within the city, primarily African American ministers. The ministers were not allowed to preach their doctrine. Rather, their mission was to sit and listen to the convicted. They were to note any of the complaints about the system, but were predominately there for counsel and support the prisoner's spiritual needs. Eventually, the jail began holding Sunday services, with ministers alternating each week. That jail ministry still exists today, under the leadership of Dr. Adams, pastor of Hartford Avenue Baptist Church.

One person I fondly remember is Margarite Smith. She was a beautiful woman, and was the wife of the manager of the basement of Hudson's. They were members of the Presbyterian Church. Margarite was a volunteer for Equal Justice Council, and had never been inside a jail before. I persuaded her to go into the jail with me one time, as a part of the jail ministry program. She struggled with her fears as we entered the jail. But once she experienced it, and saw what hope and inspiration she could bring to those in such horrible conditions, she became very active with the jail ministry on a day-to-day basis.

It takes a great deal of inner strength and courage to overcome your fears. Most times, it will be to your benefit, and to the benefit of others.

Finally, Dr. Warren's report was published. Colleges across the country requested copies. A preliminary report that had analyzed 787 misdemeanor cases during the period of September to December of 1969 had been released on March 10, 1970, to the media, the judges of Recorder's Court, and other leading citizens of the community. Two issues were identified. The first was the individual biases of the judges toward race and social class. The second was the institutional racism reflected in sentencing, bonding, and availability of quality defense counsel.

The final report examined a total of 3,625 misdemeanor cases that were observed between September 1969 and April 1970. Some of the statistical findings included:

* African American defendants received a sentence of only a fine half as often as white defendants.

* For the charge of simple larceny, African American male defendants were sentenced to jail twice as often as white male defendants, and received a sentence of only a fine one-third as often as white male defendants.

* For firearms violations, white males received a fine only sentence four times as often as African Americans. African Americans received jail only sentences for   this offense twice as often as whites.

* In the absence of an attorney, bail was set at below $1,000 for 41.7% of white defendants, and for 27.4% of African American defendants.

* A jail only sentence was rendered for defendants wearing...

coat and tie	8.3% of the time.
sport clothes	17.3% of the time.
work clothes	24.2% of the time.

* Persons with coat and tie received larger fines but shorter jail sentences than defendants in other attire.

On March 10, 1970, the preliminary report, as I mentioned, was released to the public. The 788 cases analyzed after the preliminary report was released showed some positive change in Recorder's Court behavior.

* Courtroom noise dropped from 2 out of every 5 cases to 1 out of every five cases.

* Guilty decisions for African American defendants dropped 15%, and dropped 9% for white defendants.

* There was a 5% increase in dismissals for African American defendants.

* Jail sentences of 60 days or longer decreased by 16% for African Americans, and 23% for white defendants.

My involvement with Equal Justice Council was spiritually rewarding for me. I gained a better understanding of the problems within the judicial system, and it opened the door for me to meet many wonderful people. It also caused me to consider a run for public office.

CHAPTER NINE
Women: Their Concerns And Advancement

In 1969, I decided to run for City Council. I had campaigned for so many people throughout my life; I felt it was time to campaign for myself. I had a better understanding of the problems of the city, through my work at Equal Justice Council. Lorraine Thomas, a Republican woman, helped run my campaign, and I met many people as I would walk door to door after work. It was challenging, because I could not give up my position at Equal Justice Council to campaign full time. I enjoyed the work and needed the money. God must not have thought I was ready. Or maybe it was preparation for something bigger. I never questioned God's direction for me. I went ahead and did His work, to the best of my ability. But in 1969, the best of my ability resulted in achieving 138,641 votes. The nine highest vote-getters won seats on the council, and my total was ranked 15th.

By the end of the campaign, I was out of gas. I took a few days off and went to Toronto, where I secluded myself in a hotel room, read spiritual literature, and returned physically, emotionally, and spiritually refreshed.

After I returned, an official from Wayne County Community College asked me if I would consider representing the 2nd district, on the Board of Trustees for Wayne County Community College. There was a vacated seat that I would be appointed to initially, but then I would have to run for the seat at the following election. I decided to accept the appointment, and won the election in 1970.

I was to serve as a trustee for a term of two or three years. I remember one of the major issues of concern was the building of a campus on the East Side of Detroit.

It was suggested to me, by one of the board members, that I should consider pursuing my Master's Degree at Wayne State University. It felt like the right time to do this, so here I was, the humble child from Black Bottom, pursuing a Master's Degree, while working for Equal Justice Council as its director, and serving as a trustee for Wayne County Community College. I was also a member of the National Council of Crime and Delinquency, and a member of the State Committee to end crime. The latter commitment caused me to travel all over the state to observe what was being done in different cities regarding crime.

With all of this activity, could things become any more hectic for a woman of 54 years young?

*****

In July of 1971, Councilman Robert Tindal, who was also director of the NAACP, took ill and died, leaving a vacant seat on the Detroit Common Council. The City's charter specified that in the event of a vacancy, a general election would be held to fill the seat. This was to occur during the 1972 general election, and promised to be extremely publicized because it was to be a one on one run-off between the top two vote-getters in a May primary election.

Women, particularly those active in the UAW and AFL-CIO, began encouraging me to consider running for office, after Councilman Tindal took ill, but before he passed. Millie Jeffrey, the first director of the Women's Department of the UAW, and assistant to president Walter Reuther, provided the strongest encouragement. She called me one morning, asking me to run for the office. I told her that I couldn't think about that while the man was still alive. She said, "God save the king, long live the king!" She said that when he did pass, there would not be much time to make a decision, and time would be crucial in organizing a campaign.

I hung up the phone, and took a serious look at my life. I already had an unsuccessful run for council. I was working as the director of Equal Justice Council. I was committed to my work as a member of the National Council on Crime and Delinquency and on the State Committee to end crime. I was a Wayne County Community College trustee. I was pursuing my Master's Degree in social work at Wayne State University. I was also still very active in Reverend Dr. Ann Ryan's church, Divine Temple of Mental Science. I would have to diminish or end my involvement with a number of these activities in order to put forth a serious campaign for the open city council seat.

I talked to Reverend Ryan about it. She encouraged me, and together we prayed. I approached Father Kern, from Most Holy Trinity Catholic Church, who I knew through his work in helping poor people and in his support of unions. He encouraged me, and together, we prayed. Then, I approached Martha Jean "the Queen" Steinberg. She had encouraged me to run in 1969, and once again, offered her support.

I decided to run.

*****

Forty-eight candidates sought the single seat on the city council. And I had never encountered such viciousness in my life. I didn't expect this. In 1969, there were only 18 candidates that ran to fill all nine seats. With the extreme competition, came extreme nastiness between the candidates. It was dangerous just to go to work each day. People would walk behind me and threaten me.

People threw away campaign literature that I would leave posted or displayed. Men who were running for the office behaved differently toward me. African American candidates would harass and verbally attack me in the open. White candidates attacked me behind my back.

Many of them ridiculed me about my legitimacy as a candidate. They'd taunt me by saying, "Who are you to run? You're poor. You're black. You're a woman." I would turn and respond. "I may be poor. I may be black. And I may be a woman. But beside all that, I will win this election." This would cause them to back down, for a little while.

I cannot and will not talk about those bitter moments that I faced while running the campaign - or any campaign. My memories of them are not clear and accurate because I seek the positive in situations. I have dismissed those ugly periods within campaigns, and have worked through whatever emotional pain they bore upon me. The important thing for me is to maintain my focus on that which I was fighting for.

Robert Millender was my campaign manager. But Dottie Battle became my assistant who did the lion's share of the work. Dottie was a Detroiter who had been a writer for African American newspapers across the country. She moved to California to work as an editor on scripts for television shows. She had come home to Detroit on vacation, to visit her brother, Charlie Battle. Charlie was running for another public office. I was in my campaign headquarters, working with the staff, when she and Charlie stopped by. I was in need of a press release to be written, and no one in the office was blessed with that skill. Dottie asked me what I wanted, and I told her. She sat down at the typewriter, and in a matter of minutes, the press release was complete. She was intrigued about the idea of an African American woman being elected to a city council seat for a major city, and felt that this was a challenge worth becoming involved in. She flew back to California to resign from her position. She gathered her belongings and moved back home to Detroit to assist in my campaign. We hit it off well, and worked side by side through this run-off campaign, and beyond.

I had hired a public relations firm to help me, and they provided me with a slogan that I used for this and later campaigns. You Trust Her. This slogan appeared on everything advertising my candidacy - from billboards to bumper stickers - in my campaign colors of pink and blue.

For every person who was out there trying to intimidate and discourage me from running for office, more people were getting caught up in the fervor of supporting a new voice and vision on Detroit's City Council. An African American woman's voice and vision.

When the May, 1972 run-off election was complete, the top two candidates were to run head to head, and the public would decide in November, 1972 which of the candidates would fill the vacant city council seat. I secured the top spot, with 68,221 votes. My opponent was Jack Kelly, who was the Deputy Commissioner of the Buildings and Safety Engineering department of the City, and had earned 59,519 votes. An African American woman against a white man. Racial overtones began to take shape. However, I chose not to make race an issue. As I was quoted in the Detroit News, it was my hope that the citizens would vote for the candidate on the basis of devotion to the city, merit, and ability to represent all segments of the community.

Everyone knew it was going to be a close election. In 1969, when I finished with 138,641 votes, Kelly had earned over 48,000 votes more than me, which earned him 11th place, two spots away from a seat.

It had been brought to my attention that the building inspectors were not doing their jobs. Jack was the head of the Building Department, and it reflected his inability to manage the department. African Americans would move into a building and either the inspectors did not do the job, or blindly passed a building even though it was in such decay. I spoke to Bill Haney, an African American television personality, about this, and he said that if I could bring him proof, he'd do a feature on it. So, I did. We went out to a few sights around Second Boulevard, where a building had passed the inspection, however sewage was floating in the basement. The story aired on a Sunday, and from it, I gained more support.

I did not receive the financial support that other candidates would. Instead, I went to the people. My relationship with many of the churches in the city also brought a great deal of support.

On election night, we held a victory party at the Detroit Hilton Hotel. Kelly held his victory party at the Leland House. It was that close.

My campaign committee presented me with two pieces of paper. On one was my victory speech, the other, my concession speech. I threw them both down and said, "I'm not saying any of this. I will win, and I'll speak from my heart." They looked at me like I was crazy.

I left the party with a friend of mine, Francine Albertson, who had flown in from New York to be with me during this experience. We retired to the suite we had reserved. The election was still undecided, and I thought I'd get some sleep because there was no guaranty they'd have the final result, even by morning. The press followed us, pressuring me to concede. "Why don't you give up, Mrs. Henderson?" they asked. "You're 6,000 votes behind." I replied. "I don't need to give up. Come back tomorrow, and I'll be 6,000 votes ahead." I closed the door behind them and went to sleep.

The next day, the Detroit News reported the shift. With 32,000 absentee ballots to count, and 86 precincts still to report, I had a 10,000 vote lead. The press waited outside my hotel suite and asked me how I knew I'd win. I told them that they relied on polls and predictions, whereas I relied on the truth. The truth I relied on was that I could count on the people of Detroit to make the right choice.

When all the votes were counted, I accumulated 170,598 votes over Jack Kelly's 163,189. It was a victory for the citizens of Detroit. The people - black, white, yellow, red, male and female - stood up and were counted. They stood in my corner, and I am still so extremely grateful for their support.

On Monday, November 27, 1972, City Clerk George Edwards swore me into office. The 500-seat auditorium was nearly filled. Reverend Ryan sat in the front row. I spoke briefly afterwards, pledging to focus my efforts on the physical deterioration of the city, such as housing, and on the personal deterioration, such as the crimes we commit against each other. I pledged to bring a woman's point-of-view to the council table and to the issues of the city. So many people wanted to personally congratulate me on that day, it made me late to my first council meeting.

My victory had made national news. I was the first African American woman to win a seat on the city council of a major American city. Women from across the country were contacting me, asking me how I did it. I was offered many speaking engagements following my victory, but I had to turn them down. I had to adapt to my new position, as well as prepare to campaign for the November 1973 election of the full council.

SWEARING IN AS COUNCILWOMAN HENDERSON WITH CITY CLERK
JAMES BRADLEY – EITHER 1974 or 1978.

*****

I must not forget to express my gratitude to Ms. Betty Phillips. At the youthful age of 55, I ran for and won a seat on Detroit City Council. But I was also attending Wayne State University. Betty Phillips was the head of the department of social work at Wayne, and she was determined to encourage me to finish my education. Her loyalty and love was a source of peace and healing through this challenge. She used every means possible to encourage me. I would visit her home and have breakfast with her, and she'd further help me understand social work, both in the classroom and at the city council table.

*****

The council was now made up of Ernest Brown, David Eberhard, Nicholas Hood, Carl Levin, Billy Rogell, Phillip Van Antwerp, Anthony Wiezbicki, and myself. Mel Ravitz was the president. In taking office, my eyes were opened. The council was only a part-time council. I became reacquainted with Mel Ravitz who had been a supporter and had named me to a cable television commission before I was elected to council. Carl Levin and I worked together on making the council more involved with the growth and development of the city, and sought to change its status from a part-time position to a full-time position. But, no sooner had the 1972 election finished, the city council, as a whole, would be up for election in 1973. The coalition of women that had helped me run in 1969, and grew to help me win in 1972, would come together again, and emerge as a powerful organization.

*****

The Women's Conference of Concerns began as a gathering of women who had decided on meeting and discussing matters affecting women and their role in politics every Wednesday night. They were my inspiration for running in 1969. Because of my job as director of Equal Justice Council and membership to the Michigan Council on Crime and Delinquency, I learned a lot of information that I was sharing with people during my 1969 campaign. A lot of issues for and about women were also a part of the discussions. Because there was great concern about ongoing issues and a desire to help bring about changes, I decided to begin holding weekly meetings.

Alberta Blackburn contacted Earlene Morris. Earlene and her husband, Ernest, owned the Morris Child Development Center. Alberta invited Earlene to meet with me and others. We were talking about my (1969) campaign, and about how small the office space was to hold our meetings in. We needed space, we needed money, and we were listing all the other things we would need, when Earlene offered her building as a potential meeting place. We weren't familiar with Morris Child Development Center, so someone suggested visiting the place to see if it was suitable. To our pleasant surprise, the Morris' offered a lot. Their buildings extended from 18001 to 18079 Wyoming. So we met in 18061 Wyoming at first, in their Prayer Room. I don't know why they chose their Prayer Room, but it was appropriate. As we were beginning to form a formal organization, God was in the center of it, too. Eventually, our membership grew too large for the Prayer Room, and we moved into what the Morris' referred to as Building Three, and then finally into Building Two, which held our meetings for over a decade. It was interesting, at first, because it was a child development center. We started out by sitting in little children's chairs, or sat on the floor. Eventually, the organization grew out of its infancy, into a powerful coalition of women.

The women came from all walks of life. There were some very well-to-do women, and there were some very poor women. There were professionals, laborers, and housewives. There were lawyers and law students. Teachers and students. Young adults and senior citizens. There were women of many colors and cultures, from various religious backgrounds. There were Detroit residents, and suburban residents, and even some members were from outside the state of Michigan and the United States. They were all angels.

One night, we had a meeting that was so well attended that we had no space to put everyone. People had to stand. The meeting featured a delegation that had come from one of the South Sea Islands. They were in Detroit, and had heard about our organization and chose to attend our meeting. They wanted to be a part of this unity movement, and we enjoyed socializing with them after the meeting.

When I won the 1972 election, my focus turned to my role as a city councilwoman, so I left Victoria Banks in charge of the Women's Conference of Concerns, to keep it alive. With another election to come, they helped me with my campaign, and also we set another goal.

Coleman Young was a senator in the Michigan legislature. He called me one day, to get my thoughts about his running for mayor. He was concerned because if he chose to run, and lost, he would also lose his seat in Lansing. He wanted to protect his senate seat, but still run for mayor. I told him that he couldn't run for office with two minds. "If you run, run to win. You can't win if you're also concerned about the senate job. So, turn it all loose and run to win the mayor's job."

The Women's Conference of Concerns adopted Coleman Young's campaign for mayor, as well as my re-election campaign. We realized that we needed to have a mayor that would address the problems and concerns of the citizens of Detroit, and he promised to do that.

*****

As I mentioned earlier in this book, I came to know Coleman Young during my childhood. My earliest recollection of Coleman and his family was while I was around 11 or 12 years old, living on the 2100 block of Maple Street, near St. Aubin. His father was a hefty fellow, and was a tailor. Coleman had a couple of sisters, and I remember watching the youngest girl riding swiftly down the street on her brand new tricycle. We never played together, Coleman or his sisters and I, but their family was known due to their standing in the community. His cousins owned Young's Bar B Que.

We then moved to a large, four story home on the 2700 block of Maple Street. My mother, sister, and I, my Aunt and her husband, and Mrs. Mann and her two children shared it. Remember, this was back during the depression. We were living pretty well for that period, and God was certainly taking care of us. Every person on the block took care of each other back then, too. If I went out, everyone on the block could tell you what time I had left, who I was with, what I was wearing. But this moved us away from the Young family.

It was when I went to Eastern High School where Coleman's and my path met again. That's when I'd walk to and from school with my friends, and we wouldn't associate with the boys on the way to school. We would walk and talk with them on the way home, especially by Elmwood Cemetery where we'd get the boys to pick us flowers. Coleman and I were not what you would call good friends. We were just in the same group of high school students who walked together. My impression of him then was that he was strong and tough, and not very friendly.

After high school, we became friends with the same groups of people, and faced the same kinds of issues. He was vocal as I was about unions. I felt very passionate about the need to have people, especially African Americans, join with the UAW and AFL-CIO. Still, Coleman and I were not what you would call close friends. We just traveled in the same circle of friends.

As I mentioned earlier, he was one of the bodyguards for Paul Robeson when Paul stayed at my home. Coleman also was amongst those of us trying to persuade Sunnie Wilson to allow Paul to speak on his stage.

Coleman and Reverend Charles Hill were both brought before the House of UnAmerican Activities Committee, and they both stood tall and proud against Senator McCarthy and his questioning. I was proud of them. And, Coleman and I were selected as Michigan representatives of the Henry Wallace campaign of 1948. Coleman never attended any of the board meetings.

Coleman was becoming the hero for people who felt disenfranchised by the ugly things that were going on in the country. He was constantly under attack by those who were against African American leadership. He was very active in the progressive field. I was active as well, but I felt attack more from those within my inner circle of friends and neighbors. People were afraid to get too close to me. I was too political. Dangerously political, from their point-of-view. I'm still political today, because I really want to see justice done in America and in the world. I want an end to the activities that go on behind closed doors to destroy minority groups.

In 1964, Coleman ran for the state senate. Within the district that he was running, he would hold conferences where he would educate people about the issues involving them and the City. One of the people who helped on his campaign was a social worker named Maryanne Mahaffey. This was my first introduction to her.

Once or twice, Coleman came to my house, to find out what I was doing, since I was down the road from his district. We would chat informally, and I explained to him that I was eager to get out there and do some work, but this was during a particularly difficult time for me, personally. So all I could do was wish him luck. He went on to win the seat in the Michigan Senate.

We always knew each other, and had a lot of respect for each other, because we knew what each other was doing. We were both actively engaged in fighting for what we believed in.

He was one of the first people I called on when I decided to run for City Council in 1972. He was in the senate at the time, and I asked for his support. "Why not? You've been out there ever since I can remember." He agreed to support and endorse me. So, when he decided to run for mayor in 1973, our longtime respect for each other and his support of me during my campaign, made it easy for me to help support him.

PHILLIP, PATRYA, ANN, COLEMAN YOUNG, & I

*****

Running for election again, the unions still were reluctant to support me. Particularly financially. Fortunately, I had a number of friends within the rank and file that supported me. In particular, Millie Jeffrey and Olga Madar.

Olga Madar was the vice president of the UAW. She hosted a rally at her home, supported by the 13th District Women's Democratic Caucus, in August. Over 400 women turned out, including a surprise guest speaker - Gloria Steinem. Gloria Steinem was nationally known as the editor of Ms. Magazine, and a leader in the women's liberation movement. She called my run-off election victory against Jack Kelly a "phenomenon." "In Detroit, 54 percent of the women voters turned out, more than any other city in the nation. Erma, not McGovern and Nixon, was the reason," she told the crowd.

GLORIA STEINEM

This was a time in history when women were beginning to emerge and become empowered. From my first campaign in 1969, one of the things I had learned was that even in campaign financing, women were short-changed as compared to men. I may have had a better chance of winning if I had received equal contributions as the male candidates, particularly from the UAW. Truly, part of the reason I may have been under funded in 1969 was that my campaign manager was Lorraine Thomas, a woman who was also a Republican. However, we were an all-woman team, which may have been an influential factor. To their credit, the UAW advanced certain women into their higher positions, like Olga Madar and Millie Jeffrey. Unfortunately, the women did not control the purse strings, and therefore it seemed that for every $500 the UAW would contribute to a male candidate, I would receive maybe a couple hundred dollars. This was true in this campaign as well.

My campaign focused on many issues. Land use was an issue of concern to me. There were too many vacant areas that I sought to convert to housing, recreation, and victory gardens. This would also include the city being subdivided into several areas that would then establish land use councils, to address the concerns of the people in the area about vacated businesses or homes, zoning changes, and improvement projects. I supported homesteading, that would allow the city to give qualified housing candidates land for free or a nominal charge, to bring a building up to standards, and agree to live on the property for a period of time. I was concerned about crime, physical and emotional health, employment, and women's issues.

My campaign colors of blue and pink became a regular shade during my election years. Patrya, and her daughter, Anne, helped to inspire mothers to dress their little girls in pink dresses at my speaking events. I also had the A-Team working for me. They were my Advance Team. Louis Pettiway, Coco Shindi, Irma Jaxon, and a few others. I had a schedule of places I would speak at, sometimes three or four different locations in the city. The A Team would arrive ahead of me, pass out flyers and campaign literature, and get the people excited and ready to hear me. I would then arrive, and as I began my speech, the A Team would go to the next destination, and rally the crowd there. Louis, Dr. Leno Jaxon, (Irma's brother) and my son, Phillip, would decorate the streets with signs and Dr. Jaxon also decorated a car that he'd drive me in, while campaigning through the streets of Detroit.

And then, there were the boat rides. As a fund-raiser, we'd charter a Boblo Boat, sell tickets, and have a wonderful boat ride up and down the Detroit River. People absolutely loved them, including the captain of the ship. I'd mingle with the people who came on the boat, then make my way up to where the captain sat. I'd chat with him for a while. The captains on all the boat rides during my campaigns always seemed to appreciate it when I came up and talked to them. It made them feel a part of the celebration, and not just as the provider of the service.

It was considered to be a close race for the president of City Council. The talk of the town was that it would either be Carl Levin or myself. I had the support of the women, and my platform centered on developing the city into a dynamic metropolis, with a priority on the development of decent quality lives for the people who lived in the city. Our major investment, I felt, was not in steel, concrete, and bricks alone, but rather in the development of human lives.

One of the major newspapers decided to run an article showing the positions of myself and Carl's. I believe this may have been the determining factor. Not because of the issues printed on the page, but rather for the inference that the president of the City Council could either go to a white man or an African American woman. And it wasn't the race issue that caused the problem, but rather the possibility of elevating a woman over a man. This little side battle, mostly generated by the media, had no affect on either Carl or I. We were friends, and worked well together before and after the election, at the Council table.

The 1973 election ushered in a new era for Detroit. The City Charter revision was passed, which made the City Council a full-time job. Mel Ravitz, Phil Van Antwerp and Anthony Wierzbicki were no longer on council - replaced by Clyde Cleveland, Maryann Mahaffey and my 1972 opponent, Jack Kelly. Carl Levin became the President of the City Council. I finished third, behind Carl and Nicholas Hood, with 241,547 votes. And Detroit elected its first African American mayor, Coleman Young.

I'll never forget the Wednesday after Election Day. That evening, we held a meeting of the Women's Conference of Concerns at the Morris Child Development

Center. We were in a circle of prayer, preparing to close the meeting, when the door to the room opened, and Coleman Young and his escort of associates who helped him on the campaign, entered. He was returning to Detroit from Lansing, making a stop at our meeting. It was one of the first places he stopped after the people elected him mayor. He didn't forget those who helped him in the campaign, and he was showing his appreciation by coming to our meeting. We put our circle around him and blessed him and prayed for him. He knew that he had the support of the Women's Conference of Concerns.

I also introduced him to Alberta Blackburn and Sara Foley, who were key women in the coalition, and as women who would be interested in working with him at the Mayor's office. He had promised me that he would hire two aides from our organization to be his aides. However, he only hired Alberta. I was very hurt by this, because in the many years our lives crisscrossed, it was the first time he broke a promise. However, here again, God had a better plan. It was a blessing to me that he didn't chose Sara. Sara and Louis Pettiway became my administrative assistants when the new City Charter was made effective, and Sara became instrumental in the battle that was yet to come.

*****

By the time the 1977 election came along, I was well established and well known for my care and concern for the people. It was a done deal, with the beautiful residents of the city, that I would be president. The first African American woman president of the Detroit City Council. The people returned the love I have for them, by not only electing me president in 1977, but also in 1981 and 1985. It was surprising and even humbling to me when more citizens cast their vote for me to stay on City Council in 1981 and 1985 than they had for the popular Coleman Young to stay as Mayor. (In 1981, Coleman Young received 176,710 votes, I received 194,235 votes. In 1985, Coleman Young received 89,734 votes and I received 90,509 votes).

Photograph by City of Detroit Department of Public Information

1977 DETROIT CITY COUNCIL FORMAL PORTRAIT

*****

After the 1973 election, the Women's Conference of Concerns called its first formal meeting where we elected officers and pointed the organization into a new direction. We decided to create task forces on different areas of concern. Some of these task forces included land use, education, justice, legal aid, international affairs, youth, and senior citizens. We were trying to cover the concerns of society as a whole, with individuals who were strongly interested in the issues. The task forces would work together as a group, and report at our annual conference about the issue and what was being worked on.

Even though we were named "Women's" Conference of Concerns, there were a few male members who helped organize and participated as members. Dr. Arthur Carter, my godson, and Al Fishman, a leader in the peace movement, were among them.

The annual conference would be held at Cobo Hall, and would draw 2,000 - 3,000 people from all over the state. We would hold workshops on the second and third floor of Cobo Hall, and guest speakers would discuss a variety of social issues. I think one of the most exciting conferences for me was when Issac Hayes, the musician, came to speak to the youth. We had so many young people at that conference that we had to rent another ballroom to put them all in! To see these thousand or so young people jumping and shouting, rallying to the cry of "Let's Have Freedom Now," was touching and encouraging.

The Women's Conference of Concerns still exists today. It meets the first Saturday of every month, from 1:00 PM to 3:00 PM at the International Institute, 111 East Kirby, in Detroit. Feel free to show up if you'd like to learn more and become involved.

Today, women are everywhere. White, African, Asian, Hispanic, and of all cultures. In corporate boardrooms, political offices, and in the courts. As doctors, spiritual leaders, and even as athletes. I felt it important to participate and help the advancement of women and African Americans. And I did so not to glorify me (for, as I mentioned, I have allowed God to guide me throughout my life), but with the goal of benefiting all women and the world.

CHAPTER TEN
City Council

I thought my life was busy prior to being elected to City Council. I didn't realize how much more active I'd become as a City Councilwoman!

Because my life was involved in so many things at this time, I'm sharing with you the memories of specific events and stories that I was involved in. They may not come across in chronological order, because so many situations overlapped each other. I'm just sharing with you what I thought was significant during my many years on the Council, and leave it to the historians to put it on a time line, if they must.

*****

When I first arrived on Council, I felt welcomed, particularly by Councilman Mel Ravitz. He had placed me on the Cable Television Commission to study the possibility of bringing cable television to Detroit. This was 1972, long before the cable television industry had made its growth in our nation. Back then, some of the wealthier families in Detroit had independent satellite dishes fixed to their houses, but there was no centralized cable television system available in the city.

One of my early concerns as a councilwoman was the problem of hunger in the city. I remember, while being interviewed on a late night radio talk show, people calling in about their inability to afford food. Most were senior citizens, and they were reduced to eating dog food or cat food. The Women's Conference of Concerns had brought Bill Manning into town, a man from Texas, who taught us how to grow food by changing the soil in our own backyards by using seawater. The seawater would restore the unhealthy soil to a healthier state, so that vegetables could be grown. So through the Women's Conference of Concerns, we had him teaching classes on home gardening, so that people could grow some of their own food.

Then came the voice of a woman who helped in developing Victory Gardens throughout the city. Victory Gardens was a phenomenon from the 1940's, during World War II, and due to the hunger situation, I asked Mayor Gribbs if I could reinstate them. He gave me his blessing.

Once again, I was being interviewed on a late night radio talk show. This was outside the city, in a rural area that has likely become part of a suburb now. Anyway, I was talking to hungry citizens - from Detroit and outside the city -about creating Victory Gardens and growing their own food. A woman from Lake Orion called. She had heard what I was trying to do, and was willing to help. She told me that if I could get a couple of front-loading trucks, that she had 20,000 yards of peat moss she was willing to donate to the city for my Victory Gardens. I had no idea where I would get the front-loaders from. I didn't even know what a front loader was. But I was able to locate a couple. Detroit Edison loaned us one, and another came from an African American contractor.

I had the peat moss, but where would we store it? There was an area of the city known as Lafayette Park East, along Orleans Street. Little white crosses covered the area. That's what I called them. They were white posts, encouraging people to stay away. There were no buildings on the land. Just trees and these little white crosses. It was here that we were allowed to store the 20,000 yards of peat moss. We then allowed people to come and take as much as they needed to help start their own backyard Victory Garden.

To this day, I've never met this wonderful woman who donated the peat moss to us. It was a wonderful gift, deserving of recognition.

Eventually, the peat moss ran out at about the time Coleman Young became Mayor, and housing issues became a concern. The area became developed into low income housing once the peat moss ran out.

*****

Also during this time the Vietnam War was being waged. I wanted this cruel war to end. And I found myself in the company of a Council that was mostly of similar thought. So I brought, as one of my first resolutions, the City's endorsement of Peace Action Day. The resolution urged citizens to mourn the loss of American and Vietnamese lives lost in the war, and stated that federal, state, and local government should be focused on the needs of the country that had been ignored in pursuit of the war. The Council supported me, except Ernie Brown, Billy Rogell, and Anthony Wierzbicki. The lack of support from Ernie surprised me. I hadn't realized that he was an African American conservative, who felt that he was endangering himself by backing my position to repudiate the war in Vietnam. Eventually, he voted for the resolution (Rogell and Wierzbicki remained opposed). This was an early lesson for me in learning about the individual personalities on the Council.

*****

STRESS. I don't mean the kind of stress that I experienced on Council. Rather, STRESS was the acronym for a unit within the Detroit Police Department. Stop The Robberies, Enjoy Safe Streets. They were a plain-clothes unit of white police officers that worked to take thugs off the street. However, the officers took things further than they should have, and took it upon themselves to do anything they wanted to. They'd not only stop someone walking on the street, but they'd even walk into someone's home, without a reason. The practice was prejudicial in that if the person was an African American, that person would be confronted. If an African American walked anywhere near a white community, he would most definitely be confronted. I received calls daily from people who were frightened to death with the way the STRESS officer would walk into their home and bully the residents. In some cases, citizens (predominantly African Americans) were shot and killed.

Kenneth Cockral and I had worked on Equal Justice Council to oppose STRESS, before I was elected to Council. As a council member, I was anxious to address this issue. And again, as I brought the issue up, it was the conservative members of council who told me that it was very unrealistic to get rid of the STRESS unit, and they didn't want to bring it up.

So, when Coleman was considering his run for mayor, I asked him if he would help lead the fight to put an end to STRESS. You see, the mayor's office is the executive branch of the city, and city council is its legislative branch. It is the executive branch that has the responsibility of running the city's departments, including the police department. He would have been in the perfect position to put an end to STRESS. And he reassured me that he was already committed to the elimination of STRESS.

When Coleman was elected the following year, STRESS was one of the first things he addressed, and I worked with him on it. We held community meetings, like one we held at Ford Auditorium, to help people understand why we were getting rid of STRESS, and that it could not happen overnight because of the collective bargaining agreement between the Police Officers and the City. Within the first few months of 1974, STRESS was eliminated.

*****

Many scandals surrounding HUD took place while I was on the council.

In 1969, Governor George Romney was appointed to the Housing and Urban Development Department (HUD). He was given the authority to help finance the repair and development of low-income housing in Detroit. HUD would then sell these homes, at a price higher than they were worth, to poor African Americans and others. The homes were improperly repaired, and people began abandoning them, unable to live in them.

This became front page news. HUD's first response was to red-line areas within the city where they would make the repairs, sell to low-income individuals, but would not guarantee the mortgage. When this policy became public, HUD, again, was caught in a bad light. It claimed that such a policy was not in place, and then, withdrew the policy.

To improve its image, in February of 1972, HUD announced its "Vestpocket Rehabilitation Program." This program would rehabilitate and offer for sale, some 600 to 1,000 deserted homes. This made the front page of the paper. But then, in a small classified advertisement three months later, it cancelled the program.

In May of 1972, it was revealed that HUD's 1971 policy of refusing to insure the mortgage on homes that were not inspected was not being followed on homes HUD sold from their own inventory.

In June of 1972, HUD announced another big plan. This time, they were going to create a 250-person Detroit Housing Management Task Force, to act on the large inventory of HUD-owned homes. This cost the taxpayers $2 million, and a year later, there was no showing of accomplishment.

These HUD homes were not the sturdy homes I grew up in. These were very cheaply and quickly built homes that were of very low quality. Moving furniture within the home would cause damage to the house. The landowners would then lure poor African Americans out of their durable homes and apartments, into purchasing or renting these homes, at a price above their value.

It also took long periods of time before a person interested in a HUD home could purchase one, and neighborhoods waited years before a vacant homes would either be rehabilitated or demolished, or vacant land would be cleaned up. Vacant property can quickly become home to drug dealers or other crimes. HUD had several employees either indicted or convicted of crimes, and was otherwise incompetent to handle the job of repairing and maintaining these homes. This was a major problem throughout the city, and lasted for many years, while I was on council. Every day, as a council, we would address the issues brought by landlords and tenants.

The issues regarding HUD, also overlapped my fight against redlining.

*****

I mentioned my disappointment in Coleman Young hiring only Alberta Blackburn, leaving Sara Foley behind, after promising me he'd hire them both. That rejection by him turned out to be especially helpful in our fight against redlining.

The term "red-lining" came from the practice of insurance companies identifying geographic areas, or human characteristics, that would determine if the individual would be sold homeowners or auto insurance, and would also determine the rate. In other words, the insurance companies could do as they pleased. They could deny a person insurance if they lived in the wrong neighborhood, or were of the wrong race, sex, age, or marital status. This would force people to seek out high-risk plans, which would come with high premiums.

This discrimination was not just of urban African Americans. It affected lower class rural whites. For example, Alex Kotlowitz of The Lansing Star reported the following excerpt from one insurance company's underwriting manual:

"There is the type who has never lived anywhere but in a rural area. He commutes to an industrial plant, does odd jobs, lives on relief or lets his wife make the living. You can usually spot his place. Sometimes in the summer he can be seen sitting on his front porch without his shirt. He is not a good risk."

Sara Foley had heard about a conference in Chicago that she thought the Women's Conference of Concerns should consider attending. It drew a great deal of interest, and five carloads of women drove out to Chicago. It was an inspirational adventure because here were all these women, with not a lot of money between them, making this trip. They had to sleep and eat in their cars, and crowded a hotel room or two, in order to attend the conference. The information they returned with shed light on the Michigan insurance company's practice of redlining.

This began an investigation by us. We learned that these practices kept people down, as second-class citizens, because the banks were involved, too. If you were in one of these redlined neighborhoods, or were one of these redlined individuals, you could not get loans to improve your property. We gathered information, documenting incidents within neighborhoods of excessive premiums and denied coverage or loans.

In 1977, I formed the Statewide Coalition on Redlining and Neighborhoods. As the news of our findings were getting out, we gained the support of many, such as the unions, churches, and other social organizations. We held a conference that drew about 1,200 people, and took action by petitioning Lansing. Through Sara's efforts, she was able to have the head of the State Senate and State House of Representatives appoint me as the representative on the committee that would write the laws against red-lining.

Success was partially achieved in 1977. The Michigan Legislature passed Act 135, making it illegal for a credit granting institution to deny a loan application or vary the interest rate or maturity date or percentage of down payment required, due to racial or ethnic characteristics or trends in the neighborhood where the home was located, or on the age of the structure on the real estate proposed as security. This was a huge first step, because the banks were part of the problem. The other part was the insurance companies.

Governor Miliken supported me in this fight, and made it known that it was his fight as well. He called me on my private line at the office, and provided me with a woman from his office who assisted me. And there were the many people I did not meet, who helped support me. They were the majority of citizens throughout the state who, when presented the truth, helped fight the just cause. Many people around the state contacted their state representatives to tell them that Michigan wanted an end to red-lining.

And while taking the fight to Lansing, I found myself introduced to the person known as a lobbyist. I had always heard the word "lobbyist" and I didn't know what that really meant. I had assumed that they were people who represented some group, like a company or special interest group, and that they would come before congress and share their side of a position that was before the legislature. I didn't know that they were strong, imposing, and threatening characters, and a reflection of the negative side of what I was fighting for. As I looked into their eyes, I could see they were trying to drive fear into me, in order to come around to their point of view. I would meet them behind closed doors, there in Lansing. Many of my friends would ask me, "Why are you meeting with those lobbyists?" I would respond, "Because I have to know where my enemy is coming from."

The lobbyists were a strange delegation of men who looked handsome and intelligent, but who had strong minds that would fight for the banks and insurance companies. I would listen to them, and walk out, expressing my gratitude for their concerns. I wanted to at least give them a chance to tell me their position.

Many times, people don't want to hear what the enemy has to say against them. But if you don't listen to your enemies, you don't know what they are thinking, or understand the deeper story behind their position.

Again, my spiritual teachings taught me that God was fighting this battle, not me, so I wasn't angry with them. I was marching forward with the idea that God was carrying me through this.

And the day came, when the Essential Insurance Act was passed. The Act put an end to discrimination in the purchase of auto and homeowners insurance, based on race, age, sex, or marital status. Rather, rates would be determined based on the factors an individual could control. In the case of auto insurance, this meant a person's driving record, commuting mileage, vehicle design and safety, and cost of repair or replacement. In the case of home insurance, this meant such factors as the size of the home, construction materials, repairable defects, distance from a fire hydrant, and even smoking habits.

Governor Miliken presented me the pen that he signed the legislation into law with. It was a victory for the people of the state of Michigan.

Unfortunately, the laws, over the years, have been weakened, particularly due to the insurance bureau's unwillingness to enforce the law.

It is still amazing to me the kind of change that can be achieved when five car loads of women from Detroit, attend a conference in Chicago.

In the spirit of the "I am," that I believe is within each of us, it is important that we realize that "I am a person capable of contributing to positive change." Read that sentence again.

"I am a person capable of contributing to positive change."

We must always let love abide. Our scriptures say to love your enemies. I learned to love my enemies, and that was the hardest thing I had to do. It was what I knew was right, and it protected me. I knew that if I hated them, I would not win. No matter what they said to me, or how much they may have desired to spit in my face, I would just smile and say to myself, "God bless you. Peace be with you."

Reverend Dr. Ann Ryan's words inspired me, and will inspire and guide you. She told me that if I desired justice and peace and order and love, I was apt to win any battle that I started because I would be fighting the battle where the people, not myself, were the beneficiaries of the victories.

*****

I spoke about my continuing education at Wayne State University, and how I was grateful for Betty Phillips' help in keeping me focused on my studies as well. The day did come when I graduated with my master's degree in social work. In fact, within the same week, I graduated, Patrya graduated from Wayne County Community College, and Anne graduated from the Center for Creative Studies. The infinite spirit of God guided and protected us, as we undertook the challenge of school, and achieved our goals.

GRADUATION DAY!!!

*****

In 1974, I became an ordained minister of the Divine Temple of Mental Science. Patrya was ordained on the same day. This was the church that Reverend Dr. Ann Ryan built, located at 7401 Mack Avenue.

Dr. Ryan's health was failing, and she was residing in a nursing home at the time. But I could not consider becoming ordained at the church she built, without seeing her. So I went and bought her some nice clothes, and kept them with me until the day of the ordination. I had often bought her clothes and had taken them to her, but nursing homes in those days were very suspect, and some of the new clothes I bought for her would disappear within the week, after making their way to the laundry.

Dottie Battle, Mary Robinson, and I went to the nursing home the morning of the ordination, and dressed Dr. Ryan up so nicely, she looked like a queen. Unfortunately, she was not well enough to go. But I carried the image of her, beautifully dressed, in my mind during the ceremony.

As I was getting ready to participate in the ordination, I saw Patrya sitting there. She had been having some rocky times in her life at this point. Then, an idea occurred. Because I took a majority of the classes when she was younger, and because I didn't have a place where she could go, Patrya had attended many of the required classes with me. So I reached out to her, and had her join me in being an ordained minister. I thought this was the best thing for me to do to help her create a new direction in her life, and to dedicate her to her purpose as a leader and a healer. I knew she had it in her.

The ordination was special to me. Dr. Ellis conducted the ceremony, and my teacher and inspiration, Reverend Ryan, was in my thoughts and heart. Thelma Henderson - the second wife of my ex-husband, George Henderson - and their daughter, Emma, were in attendance. Orlo Sauer, the man who guided me into healthy eating, was present. It was a special day, with deep meaning for me, as I took on the mantle of ministry.

Indeed, I was on Detroit City Council at the time. I would not allow religious discussion at the council table. But becoming a minister magnified the importance of my spirituality, and this shaped and formed my decisions while in my elected civic leadership position.

*****

An interesting incident occurred when I complained about something, either in the newspaper or at the council table. It wasn't something I was initiating as a plan at the time. It was just something that came out of me, which created an interesting result.

After a city council meeting, I returned to my office. I was rather tired from the meeting, but was surprised to find some men waiting for me in my office. When I walked in, and looked at them, I asked what it was I could do for them. They introduced themselves as representatives from Detroit Edison and Michigan Consolidated Gas. They sat at a table in my office, and I joined them.

"We just came to tell you that we like your idea designed to improve both Edison and Michigan Consolidated Gas."

"What do you have in mind?" I asked. They asked me what I had in mind. Then, I remembered the comment I had made.

I thought that it would be beneficial for the citizens of Detroit, and Detroit Edison and Michigan Consolidated Gas, to open branch offices all over the city, where people could resolve matters about their electric and gas bills closer to home, rather than having to come downtown and go to one office or the other. All of this just came out of me, but it wasn't from me. Again, I have to attribute it to God guiding me and using me.

So, I told them what I wanted to see. "I'd like to see several satellite offices where people lived, so they could go and pay their gas and electric bill, and maybe their water bill, too, with a computer link up with Lansing to know who was on welfare, what their status was, in regard to their ability to pay the bills. This would be more convenient than making everyone go to the single downtown office to take care of their bills. They looked at me, and were busy writing everything I said. They assured me that they would discuss the idea, and get back with me.

Well, a couple weeks later, these same men appeared in my office again. They laid out drawings of the city, with areas highlighted where an office would be set up, like at Seven Mile and Gratiot, and in Highland Park, for example. Detroit Edison and Michigan Consolidated Gas thought this was a major accomplishment, so they approved it.

When the first satellite office was completed, on West Seven Mile Road, I went out to see it. That's when I decided to include the Water Department into the partnership. It was satisfying seeing the cooperation of Edison and MichCon, and their agreement to do this, and not having to go through city council to have it approved. However, to add the Water Department required city approval. And it was a royal battle. I think Mayor Young didn't like the idea of having to give in to me on the issue, but we finally agreed to have the Water Department as a part of that partnership.

This was my first experience of how I thought things should be done with computers. At that time, computers were nothing like they are today, but still could provide useful services. A person at the office could punch in a person either by address or social security number, and find out if they were on welfare and if they were getting help from the state. It would provide the utility with information on the customer, and the customer could make payment arrangements at the localized office. This would prevent citizens from having their utilities shut off.

I also had a good relationship with Michigan Bell. They had an African American president at the time. I was attending their annual banquets as a guest or speaker, and worked with the company to foster good service and fair payment plans for customers, so, again, the phone service would not be arbitrarily cut due to missing a payment.

I'm telling you these things because they occurred during my time on city council, but they were not city council matters. They were Erma Henderson matters. They were matters I felt were important to help the citizens of Detroit.

So, with all these matters demanding my attention, pulling me every which way, I should have been fatigued. But I wasn't.

First of all, I had come to learn how to eat for my health. I had met Orlo Sour back when I was working for Equal Justice Council. He and his wife owned and operated a health food store at the Six Mile Road and Woodward area. He was a German fellow. I learned about his store and went to visit it. He was hesitant with me, as I asked him about the right foods to eat. But we became good friends. He found out that I was dedicated to the causes he was dedicated to, like the elimination of prejudice in the criminal justice system, STRESS, and red-lining. He supported me in changing my diet to eat only that which was healthy, and only at the proper times, to which I still live by.

In the morning, from wake-up to noon, I eat only fruit. Nothing else. Then, during the afternoon is when I would have carbohydrates - mostly in the form of vegetables and salads. No potatoes. No tomatoes. Then, for dinner, the protein. That would include beans. Sometimes fish, but only deep sea fish. Never lake fish. Never shellfish, for their shells housed the poisons from the sea that is not good for you. And I would never have a meal where carbohydrates and proteins mixed. The old-fashioned burger and fries or steak and potatoes are an unhealthy combination. Perhaps, in another book, I'll discuss everything he taught me about how to eat to maintain a healthy body.

Massage was another therapy that kept me rejuvenated. I spoke about treating myself to massage earlier in the book. Massage helps to stimulate the blood flow and energy flow in your body.

Prior to running for city council, I had given some thought to being trained in massage. Emma Clay was a masseuse who I knew had defeated discrimination in the massage profession. There was a massage school that received public funds, but would not allow African American women enrollment. Emma took on this challenge. She was able to break down that barrier and became a licensed masseuse as a result. But Attorney Arthur Boman, who later became a judge and supporter of my campaigns, knew me better than myself, and suggested I take the political route over a career in massage therapy.

Not only did I have a regular massage, but the profession came into view while I was on city council. There was a woman from the Law Department who was campaigning to become elected as a judge. Part of her campaign was to eliminate massage parlors. Her concern was that massage parlors were undercover operations for prostitution. She and I had a discussion about the massage profession, and I had some professional masseuses come in and talk to her about the healing power of massage. So she understood where I was coming from, and I understood where she was coming from, and together we had to figure out how best to resolve the situation so that both of our goals were achieved. Leno Jaxson, one of my loyal campaign team members, had attended this meeting. As the lawyer and I spoke, he leaned over and whispered in my ear the solution. "Keep clothes on." By creating an ordinance that allowed for licensed massage parlors to operate, and mandate that clothes must remain on the masseuse, such professional massage therapy clinics could remain open and not fall under prostitution disguised as a massage parlor.

Today, most doctors recommend massage as a relief of stress and tension in the body.

Finally, another aid in my ability to balance so many matters in my life, was walking. Particularly on Belle Isle. I would walk on the Isle every morning, sometimes joined by friends. Alberta Blackburn would often accompany me. So, too, would Martha Jean "the Queen" Steinberg. Martha was very supportive of me during these years, and I helped her establish the Home of Love, on Grand River Avenue. The Home of Love included the Joy Building for Children, and were places established to help make a difference in people's lives. I believe Mayor Young took credit for it, back at the time, however if the money had not passed through the city council, it wouldn't have happened. And it was the Queen that inspired another tradition I had established in the city.

*****

It was in 1978, during my first term as City Council President, when, on one night, the Queen and I had left Hallas' restaurant in Greek Town after attending a party in a banquet room upstairs. Her car was parked behind St. Mary's Church, and we walked in that direction. I remember the moon was big and bright in the sky. She was aware of the Women's Conference of Concerns, but being a spiritual woman, she shared a vision she had with me. Her vision was for me, as a leader of the city, to call together the people of the city for the purpose of prayer. This would manifest as an annual meeting of prayer for the city, the nation and the world. It was late, and I wanted to give it some thought.

The next day, Alberta Blackburn, the Queen, and I were walking on Belle Isle, and talked about it. We decided that it would be an annual prayer breakfast, calling it The Breaking of Spiritual Bread. We decided to hold the event at Cobo Hall, and we pulled together the names of several women who would help coordinate it. Women like Patricia Lewis, LaTrelle Powers, Barbara Turner-Mays, Marian Boyd and Mary Robinson, to name a few.

So, beginning in December of 1978, and annually every December thereafter, for the 12 years I presided over the City Council, we held a Prayer

Breakfast. We would have music from children's choirs to soloists such as Ortheia Barnes and Bessie Waters, followed by an opening invocation.

Ortheia Barnes, one of Detroit's finest voices, once owned a nightclub on Eight Mile Road. My nephew, Phillip, and his girlfriend once took me to it for dinner. But with her involvement with the Women's Conference of Concerns, Ortheia began to change, spiritually. She began referring to me as "Mother", and wanted to meet with me weekly, to learn and understand spiritual practice. She eventually sold the club, changed her focus, and became a minister. She and her husband, Bob Kennerly, founded Spirit Love Ministries, and though she still sings here and around the world, she has become a spiritual leader.

After the invocation, I would pray and break the bread, along with those in attendance at their breakfast tables. Awrey Bakery, one of the oldest bakeries in the city, baked our bread every year. They would clean their ovens prior to the baking of our bread, so that the people felt that they were being provided the most holiest of breads when they participated, and to make it a deeper spiritual experience People loved it, and came back every year. Over the course of time, people would tell me that they had spiritual experiences and healing from attending.

After the breaking of the bread, breakfast would be served. Then, we held prayers for the city. We had many representatives from various churches and religions. Baptist, Catholic, Methodist, Eastern Orthodox, and Islamic. All would offer prayers.

Like I said, people seemed to love it, because they came back year after year while I was president of the council. We would easily have 1,000 people in attendance, under one roof, with prayers from a number of religious and spiritual traditions.

CHAPTER ELEVEN
Nationally & Internationally Speaking

By winning the election in 1972 over Jack Kelly and earning a place at City Council, I was not only exposed to the causes and concerns of the citizens of Detroit, but it also opened a door that led me into the national and international community.

Once arriving on council, I immediately learned of the many connections within the elected officials community. At first, I learned about the Michigan League of Cities. This organization would consist of all the city councilpersons and mayors of every city in Michigan. There would be conferences where these elected officials would discuss the problems and various solutions that could be applied to improve their city, and a forum to band together and seek cooperation from other governmental entities.

My first experience at one of these conferences brought about the awareness that I was one of very very few African Americans. There may have been three or four of us, total. There were a few more women in the group. I believe it was at a breakfast where I suggested the idea of creating a women's division or a women's group within the body of the organization. I wanted to unite us and see if we could find common ground, to view the problems that affected our cities from a collective women's point of view. This group of women leaders would bring a perspective that could create solutions that the male point of view would not think of.

At first, I was met with great suspicion. There were so many women who were proud to have been elected, who achieved a feeling of independence, that they were hesitant to come together as a group. This was an initial obstacle to our discussions. There were also some who said that we really couldn't do that. I frankly asked them if they were saying that women cannot come together or that we don't need to come together, because men could handle all the issues, even those issues that affect women the most. They began to see that I was not suggesting this out of my own interest, but that I was just trying to create a group where women elected officials would work together for the improvement of Michigan cities. After much discussion, we agreed to form, and the first meeting of the Women's Auxiliary of the Michigan League of Cities was held.

Unfortunately, I never had the opportunity to work diligently with this group as I would like to have. I attended a few meetings, provided my thoughts and encouragement. But I also had become involved with the National League of Cities.

The National League of Cities provided a broader forum for women in government to come together. There were women from around the country who were in the National League of Cities before I, however they were from generally small cities in America. These women carried very little strength because of the small cities from which they came. However, when I was elected, and became involved, suddenly there was a woman elected official from a major city who could help bring the group of women together, and provide a voice in the overall organization.

My first experience with the National League of Cities was at their annual meeting that was held in Puerto Rico. Mayor Gribbs invited me to attend. He had chartered a plane so that many of the Michigan elected officials would attend the conference together. I was originally allowed to bring a person with me, however I wanted two people to attend. Dottie Battle and Marge Thompson were my administrative assistants, and I wanted both of them to attend, especially Marge who then became president of the Women's Conference of Concerns. Because there was room on the plane, Mayor Gribbs allowed me to bring them both.

Puerto Rico was a beautiful country, but it had its extremes between poverty and wealth that left me with a bad feeling. Our hotel was luxurious, and we stayed in a beautiful room. We had time to walk along the stunning beach, and enjoyed the dining and events that were held in the evening.

There was a city councilwoman from Highland Park who attended, who thought she could bring the women of the National League of Cities together. She invited them all to have lunch. A number of women attended and listened to her idea about coordinating a group. However, there were councilwomen from larger cities than Highland Park who weren't willing to follow her lead. The debate became heated at times, nothing was accomplished, and some bad feelings arose between the women. I thought it better to let things cool, and maybe give it a try next year.

From the hotel we were staying in, I could see a number of smaller houses clustered together, at the bottom of a hill. They looked like rows of pillboxes. Those were the people I wanted to see. I spoke to someone about it, and it was arranged for me to go.

There, children played in the streets, almost naked. They looked hungry and unkempt. It was the worst poverty I had ever been exposed to up to that point, and it made me want to cry. The women did not work, and the men were mostly servants to the luxurious estates and businesses. We talked to some of the women. They were friendly, but it made you want to cry because they did the best they could. I can still remember the eyes of their hungry little children. Mentally, physically, and spiritually, they were weak.

An incident occurred as we were driving through the neighborhood. The car came to a stop, as a little boy, almost naked, stood in the middle of the street. I got out of the car and started to approach. The child backed up a step, and then determined I was not going to hurt him. He then asked for some money.

This just tore my heart in two. If I were to participate by giving the child some money, it would further encourage him to continue to beg. The other option was to pass him by, and pray he doesn't starve. The latter option I did not want to participate in, so I gave the little boy some money. He was so happy. He smiled and was a delightful little fellow. I returned to the car, and we continued on our way, only to come to the next stop, to see more children begging.

It was the most heart-wrenching time of my life. It created in me the life-long desire to end poverty, worry, want, and pain. I never got over those experiences in Puerto Rico. I was forced to remember those scenes many years later, because I experienced more like them in other parts of the world.

I was invited to and attended a lunch at the Bank of the Commonwealth's president's home. The house was extremely lavish. I wondered about the people who were preparing the food, and whether they were servants, living sparsely, like the residents of the pill-box like houses.

*****

The following year, after I won my first full-term election, the National League of Cities annual conference was held in Houston, Texas. We were in this big hotel, and I decided we'd try to establish a women's group again.

I began by talking with councilwomen individually, explaining to them how we had to come together because many issues were confronting women at this time. The women's movement was growing, and we, as a group, could address the issues and find ways in which to address issues in our local areas. Then, I invited them to my hotel room for a group meeting. I didn't really know what to expect, whether anyone would even show up. But once the word got out, and the meeting began, my room was full of women.

They made it quite clear to me that they were not going to organize unless I was going to be the leader. I explained to them that I didn't want any office or title, because I wanted to be free to speak my mind. We agreed on a meeting time and place for that evening, and held the meeting in a conference room where there was more space. A woman from Texas chaired the meeting, and a woman from New Mexico became the first president of our group. Other officers were elected, and the Women in Municipal Government of the National League of Cities was born.

That first meeting was very vocal - after all, these were all councilwomen who weren't shy. But we settled down to business to determine what we were going to do, now that we had organized.

Jessie Rattley, from Newport News, Virginia, who was the first African American woman on the Newport News city council, and later became the first African American mayor in that city, was going to speak on the floor of the convention. She agreed to bring up a woman's issue before the assembly, to see if we could get the entire convention to support this issue in the city councils throughout the nation. She spoke before them, and the Women in Municipal Government group was recognized.

This was 1974, and Roe v. Wade had been decided in the previous year, which fueled the abortion debate. This was, and still is, a particularly important issue to a woman's right to privacy. Led by Jessie Rattley on the floor of the convention, we explained to the male leaders the importance of the issue. We were empowered by our collective voice. I think we shocked the men. They accepted us and because they really didn't understand the issue from a woman's perspective, they listened. In the end, many of them supported our proposal to support the Roe v. Wade decision.

We got that one passed, and that victory helped unite us as a group. We agreed that at each convention, we would elect officers for that year. When the convention ended, we all went our separate ways, with collective joy in our hearts at what we achieved in Houston.

Thereafter, we met for many years, and had not experienced any of the negativity that we experienced that first time in Puerto Rico and in the beginning of the Houston conference. There was a lot of prejudice in the group at those two conferences. But they began to accept my leadership, although I was not the city council president yet. I was speaking out strongly for Roe v. Wade and other issues of policy that the Women in Municipal Government supported, including health care, families and children, education, crime, and gun control.

And because we had organized, the National League of Cities had to provide us with services, such as keeping our mailing list and mailing out our materials, like the other committees.

At one of the conventions, held in Denver, Colorado, they elected me to the leadership position of the group. I was surprised. They were very loving and kind to me, and it meant that over the years, I had won their respect. I did all I could do that year to address women's issues.

Prior to the convention in San Francisco, the women discussed the possibility of getting a woman elected to the Board of Directors. It was decided that I should run for the position. However, in order to get elected, someone had to nominate me.

Coleman Young was a delegate, being a mayor. So I asked him if he would nominate me for a board position. He agreed, and made one of the most beautiful speeches I ever heard. I remember just one line from it.

"I just think that we're (the City of Detroit) the loser if you elect her, in one way, because that means she will have less time to give to us. But knowing Erma, she will probably give us equal time and work twice as hard."

I was ready to cry. I had never heard him make such a beautiful speech. He was telling them things about how he admired my work at Equal Justice Council, and many other things I did not expect him to say.

In retrospect, I understood he was also making it clear to me that the National League of Cities was mine, and that the mayor's office was his. I didn't mind.

Anyway, we shared dinner that night to celebrate my election to the board. The board position was for a two-year term. But I was excited, and the women's group was excited. I was there to represent the women.

*****

As a local councilwoman, there are many roles I played. I was deeply engaged in the needs and demands of the city. But I was also a part of this national organization that put me in touch with what other city councils were doing across the nation.

Being on the Board of Directors also provided me the opportunity to be exposed to more travel and first hand experience of projects and programs from around the nation. For example, I had the opportunity to see what a private casino looked like. The private casino was run by the state, though I don't recall which state it was that we went to. After seeing how the state ran the casino, it was how I would prefer casinos to be in Michigan. This casino was out in a secluded elaborate club-like atmosphere, well away from the city, that was also separated from a fine dining room with beautiful decor. A family could dine in the dining room, and be secluded from the casino activities. In that arrangement, they were not losing any money.

The board meetings took me to elegant places. I remember a club in North Carolina. It was absolutely one of the most beautiful places I had ever seen. A large club house. Expansive meeting rooms. The finest of food. I joked with the men on the board, "So this is what you guys do!"

I remember going to Savannah, Georgia. The Mayor took us on a tour where confederate and union soldiers had battled. We saw the old courthouse, and how rich in history the city was, and how, with federal funding and law, the once slave quarters had become housing. He also took us up the Savannah River in small boats to a castle-like estate. Food was prepared outside, and it was very good. I was eating fish at the time. I rarely ate chicken, and did not eat meat. And the fish served at this site was so good, I didn't want to try anything else. However, I did weaken a little, and indulged in some pie. It was beautiful.

These are just a sample of the trips I was permitted to take as a board member of the National League of Cities. I could work on issues from a national perspective, and during the whole period, the city of Detroit supported me. Nobody fought me about these national duties. Sometimes, newspaper people would sniff around to see what elected officials were doing, and where they were going if they were going to be out of town. But they could find nothing wrong with what I was doing, because there was nothing wrong. Locally, I was attending similar meetings with the Michigan League of Cities, most of them taking place on Mackinac Island.

At the National League of Cities, I also saw something interesting. Very wealthy people, who had won elected office, would stand and talk for hours to try to sway people to their positions. They were usually young men, who were sharply dressed and groomed, and they spoke very well. However, they were representing special interests around the country - business interests, such as oil and cement. They would take over the floor, and make it difficult for those who spoke against them to have an equal voice on the floor. Yes, they were elected officials within their community, however they represented the businesses that provided them with their donations, and not that of the community they represented.

It is a challenge to win every fight. But there were times that I knew I had to give up a fight because you can't win everything. I was really learning how to know when something isn't going to come to pass, no matter how hard I fought, and when not to give up. This experience helped empower me in my campaign to end redlining.

I also managed to bring the National League of Cities conference to Detroit. This brought many leaders from all over the country, to the city. It allowed the city to receive some good publicity, and brought in revenue to our local tourism businesses.

Overall, my experience with the National League of Cities helped me to become a better city council member for Detroit, educated me in the ways other cities handled their problems, and allowed me to help organize a powerful group of women that would defend and foster the programs and policies that would benefit women, children, and families across America.

*****

Another honor bestowed upon me by having been elected to city council was the opportunity to meet and help support the campaign of Jimmy Carter. During his campaign, he came to Detroit. Dottie Battle's brother, Charlie Battle, was a sheriff and was assigned to escort Mr. Carter around town. He was this beautiful, down-to-earth man, who was extremely special and soulful. He was definitely not a bigshot who would look down on people. Rather, he respected everyone, which in turn, earned the respect of the people.

He spoke at Cobo Hall, and met and spoke with myself and other women supporters from the Women's Conference of Concerns. An affair was being held for him on East Grand Boulevard, at a night club, and I went along. Everyone there got a chance to talk to him and get to know him.

Coleman Young arranged for him to return to Cobo Hall and speak. The shadow of the Watergate scandal over the head of President Ford, and the honesty and love that Jimmy Carter walked and talked, won the day, and Jimmy Carter became our nation's 39th president.

During the negotiation of the Panama Canal treaty, he invited a number of us Detroit supporters to the White House. Mayor Young got Henry Ford to let us use his private airplane, and we flew as a delegation to Washington DC. It was a wonderful experience. I got to meet a number of the White House press, and received a tour of the White House. This was another experience that broadened my knowledge on the nation and its international relations.

I was also a delegate to other White House conferences, including the White House Conference on Families, and the White House Conference on Economic Growth.

Jimmy Carter would deal with foreign affairs, like create good relations with China, and inspire the leaders of Israel and Egypt to establish peace between them. Yet, he was also concerned with the people of the United States. He was such a humane individual that I wondered how he ever got elected. He and his wife, Rosalynn, are such beautiful people. I was delighted and proud when I heard him recently receive the Nobel Peace Prize.

*****

My City Council position exposed me to international opportunities. Locally, I helped to foster trade between Africa and Michigan.

Betty Appleby was a part of my staff, and she helped me to find a way for the possibility of trade between African business and Michigan. We learned about the Continental Africa Chamber of Commerce, that was based in Washington DC, that had started up at some point in 1979 or 1980. Ohene Darko, a Ghanian, was the president of this organization. So we went to Washington DC to speak with Darko and the other African ambassadors, and invited them to come to Detroit. They were sincere and interested, however they could not come to Detroit on their own. Their organization was young, it was a non-profit, and therefore, they couldn't just write an expense check to cover their trip. I told them I would find a way to bring them to Detroit. First, I needed to get them to Detroit, and sought ways in which to do this. After talking to quite a number of people, one of the airlines offered to help us get the African delegation here.

Then, I had to put them up somewhere, because we were planning a week-long stay, with a three-day event to be held at Cobo Hall I spoke with some of Detroit's leading citizens who lived in spacious homes. They were not only willing to have a guest or two stay with them, but many also held house receptions for them, so that their friends and relatives had the opportunity to meet these African leaders. Also, my godson, Arthur Carter, took them out on a boat ride, on the Detroit River, to see the skyline of our beautiful city.

The delegation arrived in Detroit, and they spent seven days with us in late June of 1982. Fourteen African countries were represented, and they included Djibouti, Ethiopia, the Gambia, Ghana, Kenya, Liberia, Nigeria, Rwanda, Sierra Leone, Sudean, Somalia, Tanzania, Tunisia, and Zambia.

On June 28, 29, and 30th, we held the conference at Cobo Hall. The first day was informative. Each country's representative spoke about the natural resources, imports and exports, and investment prospects that his or her country offered. The next day, several workshops took place on issues such as agriculture, trade and development, educational and cultural programs, financing trade with Africa, technologies, and transportation. One of my fondest memories was that the State Department of Agriculture sat down with one of the ambassadors, and the two developed a trade agreement for several tons of grain to be sold to Nigeria. It was a fantastic conference that helped form the Michigan chapter of the African Partners in Trade, to which Betty Appleby was named director of, and served on for many years.

*****

In 1974, I had my first opportunity to speak before an international assembly, in another country. The opportunity took me to Helsinki, Finland, where I was representing America at the World Peace Council on Global Disarmament.

I was running a little late, my flight having arrived late. The driver who picked me up, took me to the hotel to drop off my bags and freshen up. I was then taken to the conference. There was a place for me to sit on stage, and I went up to it. Looking around, I noticed that there were many people from many different countries participating. And though there was certainly a language issue, everyone seemed to understand the speaker. It wasn't until it was my turn to speak that I noticed that I was to stand within something that was like a booth. Everyone in the audience had an earphone, and though I spoke English, everyone heard my speech in their language. I was amazed and awed by this technology.

I spoke about the need for peace in the world. Unity, peace, and healing throughout the world. I felt so humbled by the experience.

Besides this amazing technology of being able to speak in one language, and the listeners able to hear it in their language, I learned something else about these conferences, particularly those on an international level. Within a conference such as this, there was also what I call false friends. These were people who were sitting in attendance, silently paying attention, who would share a kind word with you. But they were really interested in what was going on because they supported interests that were in opposition to what the conference was about. It shouldn't be something that would make you stop attending or supporting such conferences. Just know that in any event such as an international world peace conference, there will be a handful of participants who oppose world peace in attendance.

*****

In 1975, I attended the United Nation's Conference on Women, in Mexico City. This was the first international women's conference, and it was organized by the United Nations to improve the conditions for women all over the world. Twelve platforms for action were developed, and the conference empowered women to take action within their communities. The twelve platforms were:

1.   Poverty
2.   Education
3.   Health
4.   Violence
5.   Armed and Other Conflicts
6.   Economic Participation
7.   Power-Sharing and Decision-Making
8.   National and International Machinery
9.   Human Rights
10.   Mass Media
11.   Environment and Development
12.   The Girl Child

The conference was the starting point of a decade-long examination of the equality of women to men in the areas of education, economic opportunity, wealth, health, and power.

I was invited to speak at one of the workshops at the 1985 United Nations International Conference for Women in Nairobi, Kenya. Some of the other Michigan women who attended the conference were Barbara-Rose Collins, Shirley Nuss, Edwina Davis and Congresswoman Carolyn Kilpatrick. Betty Appleby joined me. It was a wonderful experience, and I had an opportunity to speak with United Nations Under Secretary General, Lucille Mair. She was from Jamaica, and was the first woman to hold the position of Under Secretary General. It was another wonderful experience and another opportunity to meet with women from around the world, working together to balance the scales of equality throughout the world.

*****

As you can see, a position in government can afford you the opportunity to become engaged locally, nationally, and internationally. In 1985, myself, Maryann Mahaffey, Barbara-Rose Collins, Clyde Cleveland, and John Peoples were invited to Detroit's sister city in what was the Soviet Union at the time, Minsk. The City of Minsk picked up all but the airfare costs for a ten-day trip. We were impressed by the way the Minsk City Council operated. Their emphasis was on how the quality of life could improve, and they charted their course through a master plan that was frequently revisited. Their emphasis was on education, sports, and culture for their young people, to build their character and prevent crime. Their transportation system included a subway, trolleys busses, and cabs, and was something we could have learned from to implement in Detroit.

In 1988, six of us went as guests of the Montenegrin Immigrant Society, for a ten day visit of Montenegro, Mostar, Sarajevo and Belgrade, Yugoslavia.

Myself, Clyde Cleveland, Jack Martin, Marilyn Sambrano, and Marge Fishman, toured and held many discussions with the various mayors, city councils and chambers of commerce. We spent time in Titograd, where we visited an Albanian community. The Albanians were a minority within the country, and they prepared a beautiful luncheon for us.

These are just a couple of examples. I have been to many places around the world that I could write another book just about them.

Photograph published in Pobjeda

MEETING MAYOR IVANOVIC OF TITOGRAD

Photographer Unknown

OUR DELEGATION TO YUGOSLAVIA

*****

In December of 1982, I took a vacation to the island of Grenada. It is the island furthest south in the Caribbean, of the Windward Island chain. It was a small island, with a population of around 110,000 people. I thought that going to a Caribbean island in the winter would be a nice change of climate, and Grenada was an island I had never been to. Dottie Battle came with me on this vacation.

Our initial experience was not pleasant. The room in the hotel we stayed in, which was not in the major city of St. George's, was extremely buggy. You just couldn't get them to stay out of the room. So we decided that we needed to find somewhere in the city to stay.

We found an American company located there - an accounting firm - and asked the management for advice. Someone suggested a castle that rented out rooms. It was there we stayed for the remainder of our vacation. And it was luxurious! You could see the large ships and ocean liners from the porch. You could hear the music and partying of those on the cruise ships. Those ships were the playgrounds for the rich!

There was also a medical school on the island, with students from many countries that helped support the economy.

Like my trip to Puerto Rico for the National League of Cities conference, and other places I had been, there was a vast difference between the rich and the poor. However, change was being made when Maurice Bishop led a bloodless takeover of the government in 1979. He helped to organize worker's councils and a participatory government for the people of Grenada. He also emphasized and moved towards creating free education for all the children, an extensive health care program, and women's programs. He initiated the building of the airport that opened the door to tourism. But because Bishop received assistance from Cuba, the Soviet Union, and later, the Sandinistas of Nicaragua, he was labeled a Marxist.

Dottie and I attended a Christmas party there, at the castle, and the people were also celebrating the harvest of their crops. Cooperative farming was another practice Bishop brought to the people, and he was in attendance at this party. When he walked in, people hugged him. He was a very personable individual, not stand-offish or guarded, like some leaders can be.

When it was learned that Dottie and I were there - American citizens - he was led to our table. "Let me welcome you to our homeland," he said to us. We introduced ourselves, and we spent a couple minutes talking. He explained about the cooperative farming and how the country still had a ways to go to eliminate poverty, but inroads were being made. As our conversation ended, I gave him my card and told him to contact me if he ever came to Detroit. He knew Detroit was the automobile capital, and he was looking to encourage a relationship with the

United States, and was planning on visiting America. I told him that my desk was his desk, if he were ever to visit.

So we left, well rested, with a better understanding of the country. I did experience retaliation for my visit. I had taken a set of brand new luggage I bought at Hudson's on this trip, and it was torn up in Barbados, where we transferred planes to go to the U.S. I wasn't aware of the political climate at the time, and that people in the area didn't like people who had gone to Grenada. There was an attitude of disrespect for us in Barbados when we transferred to our flight to Florida, and my brand new luggage was ripped up.

The following June, Maurice Bishop was in Detroit. Representatives John Conyers and George Crockett hosted him. I pulled out all the stops, and had the auditorium decorated for his visit and address to the City Council. We didn't have a chance to really sit down privately and talk about each other's countries. He did present me with a lovely tapestry, which he said his people made for me, because they loved me. He was tickled that I did let him sit at my desk. "Mrs. Henderson," he said, "I have enjoyed every minute I have spent in your city." I asked him what his plans were, and he said that he was going to Canada after spending another couple days in Detroit. I asked him if he was being safe and careful, because the political climate was such that President Reagan was talking about Grenada as if it were Cuba. He said he wasn't afraid. He told me he was going to speak at an educational radio station the next day, while in town. I told him to be careful because this country isn't all that friendly to everyone. He told me not to worry about him.

On October 19, 1983, one of Bishop's cabinet members, Bernard Coard, who was an extreme Marxist, led a violent takeover of the government. He took Bishop and his wife, and other supporters of Bishop into prison. The people began to revolt, and attempted to free him, however Bishop and his wife were executed.

On October 25, 1983, United States Marines invaded the tiny island nation. The invasion was an atrocious act by President Reagan. I initiated, and we passed a resolution that condemned the invasion by the United States for imposing its political and military will over another nation. It was a sovereign country that was resolving its own internal differences, which caused no threat to any of its neighbors.

*****

The last international travel story I'll tell you about was when I was invited in 1986 to Desmond Tutu's enthronement as Anglican archbishop of Cape Town, South Africa. Derrick Humphries, an attorney in Washington DC who was from Detroit, and had helped me in my campaigns, arranged it somehow that I received this invitation. I was honored, and I thought I had better let Mayor Young know that I was going, otherwise he might have a fit. As it turned out, he was not invited, which didn't make him to happy with me. I offered to have him come as my guest, but I think he liked that even less.

I traveled with Derrick Humphries and the clergy from his Washington DC church. A guide showed us around the city of Cape Town, and took us to the museums. At the hotel, we were treated courteously.

It was an interesting adventure. I had heard, when I was a child in the Baptist church, of the slavery going on in South Africa, and the story of how the diamond industry was one of the country's valuable exporters. I remember being told that the mines operated from dawn to dusk. As a safety precaution (for the mining company), workers coming out of the mine were given a laxative to flush their system, and would not be allowed to leave until they defecated, to insure that the worker did not try to steal any of the diamonds.

Mayor Young did manage to get an invitation, but was to arrive a day later than us. A Detroit Free Press photographer and I were charged with the duty of picking him up at the airport. But I wanted to explore the city further, and the reporter had been assigned to Cape Town for some time, so he was able to take me to some of the sights that the tour guides wouldn't. I wanted to see where the poor lived, and he knew right where to take me.

It was a rainy day, and we drove into one of the poor sections of the city. The homes were small shacks, with paper-thin walls. We started talking to some of the women, and they invited us into their home.

The homes were no larger than a small studio apartment. They had no plumbing. They explained that there was no way they could send their children to school because there was no bus. Those that could get to school, the children were treated poorly. As I sat, listening to the family, I was crying on the inside.

As we left the house and went to the car, we saw a pregnant woman, trying to get into a civic building, but it was locked. She looked very heavy with child, and she was holding herself in such a way that it was about ready to come. I asked her where she was trying to go. She said that she was trying to get to a building not far away, to get to a doctor. We took her in our car, however, when we got there, the door was locked. I suggested that we get her into a cab and send her to the hospital. But she said, "no, no, no, no." She didn't want to go to the hospital because she didn't have any money. We asked some of the women where the hospital was, and they told us of a hospital where she could go and have the child. So, the photographer hailed a cab, and directed him to the hospital that he needed to take her to. The cab driver didn't want to do it, because she was ready to give birth, but the reporter over-compensated him, to get him to take her there. Then, we got into our car, and hurried to the airport to pick up Mayor Young.

Photographer Unknown

DESMOND TUTU & I

*****

It was a Sunday morning when we entered the Anglican church in Cape Town. Mayor Young and I were escorted into the church, to a platform where many dignitaries sat. Desmond Tutu knew us from an earlier visit to Detroit, seeking support for the release of Nelson Mandela.

The ceremony was absolutely beautiful. A youth choir sung a wonderful selection of hymns. And then, an African choir came out and simply rocked that church. Desmond Tutu was enthroned as the Arch Bishop of Cape Town, and he delivered a powerful speech.

After the service, we followed Desmond Tutu and the leaders of the church out into the street, and walked to an athletic stadium that was already full of Africans, cheering for newly enthroned Arch Bishop.

Mayor Young left later that day, but I stayed the rest of the week to tour the country. I was going to go to Johannesburg, with the Bishop I had traveled with, to their church-owned school. As we drove, there were walls along the roads that sparkled, like diamonds or other precious shavings. As beautiful as they were, I couldn't help but know that it was slave labor that built them. The roads were clear and clean, lightly traveled, with no one breaking the speed limit.

We checked into a hotel in Johannesburg for the night. The next morning, we drove to the school that was owned by the Episcopalian church, and spent the day with the students. They were from all over Africa, and were being provided the best education in order to go on to college and become leaders. In that one day's visit that we had, I met, who I consider, my adopted son from South Africa. The other kids were teasing him because he was tall and thin and was the best runner in the school. He was also one of the best students in the school. This guy became attached to me because I was making the students get off his back. They wanted him to run to win the next race for the school. But he didn't want to be a runner. He wanted to be a preacher. So, I asked him if he ever thought about running for God. He gave me a shocked expression. I told him to think about it overnight. "The school needs you and that's God." I told him to think about what God was in his mind. "How do you see God? Is God a person, or a spirit? What in your mind is God? As a preacher, you have to preach the truth. The school needs you and loves you, so you think about it."

Next day, I came back to the school because my plane was delayed because of a problem of some sort. He was not expecting me. While he was training, he saw me, and he ran towards me, his long legs running for all they were worth. He came over and hugged me and I asked him if he was running for God. "Yes I am.," he said, "I'm running for God."

Little did I expect that one day he would write to me for money to go to school. He wrote down the amount he needed, which looked like a lot of money, in their currency. Then he called me asked me to help him get to school. He considered me his adopted mother. So I took the letter to the bank, and the teller calculated how much it was. When the teller told me that it was $300, I was shocked and pleased. $300! I knew I could afford that. So I sent him the money so he could go to school. It's not like I always had $300 to send to everyone, but you do what you can and you do what you should, and you put your money where your mouth is.

Anyway, before I left South Africa, I did get to see Robben Island, where Nelson Mandela was being held in prison, from a distance. I was appalled Guards encircled the prison, which was built on this little island in the middle of a river. Crocodiles populated the river, so even if a person attempted an escape, and got by the guards, they would likely not survive swimming across the river. In February of 1990, he would finally be released.

In June of 1990, Nelson Mandela came to Detroit. Almost 50,000 people packed Tiger Stadium to see him and hear him speak. By then, I was out of City Council, and though I didn't have any input into it, I did have the opportunity to meet him at the airport upon his departure.

*****

I have always been active in allowing God to work through me, in order to make the world better for all people. Being on Detroit's City Council not only allowed me to lead in the betterment of the Detroit community, but to go beyond Detroit, helping the people of Michigan, the nation, and the world.

I know many of you know me from my days on City Council, and I hope these last couple of chapters have provided some insight as to what I felt were the most memorable and important moments and contributions of my 17-year tenure. I have left out a number of things, mainly because it would require writing an entire book just on those 17 years. Dottie Battle would have been the best person to write that book. She was there with me every step of the way, and afterwards, and I am grateful to her for her friendship. Unfortunately, she has just recently passed, over the 2003 Labor Day weekend. I sincerely miss her.

CHAPTER TWELVE
Life After Council

Photograph by Michael Kitchen

MEMORIAL PARK WAS RENAMED
ERMA HENDERSON PARK
ON NOVEMBER 2, 1989

I had traveled to several countries, and became aware of the struggles of other people. I had become involved in women's issues here, in the United

States, and I was familiar with the issues of women internationally. Governments oppressive to women and the people abroad requires a vigilant eye, just as vigilance is required here to prevent an oppressive government. All we need to do is help teach the world to understand that everyone is a human being.

Equality for women is a big issue for me. Women should be allowed the freedom to be equal to men in all things. If a woman wanted to be a firefighter, and she could show that she was a capable firefighter, then she should be allowed.

I wanted to give women the thought that they, too, could run for mayor. That, as a woman, she didn't have to reach equality only in the labor market, but also as leaders, such as chief executive officers of corporations, and as heads of government. But they had to realize that they had to have the drive and determination, and of course, the financial support.

When I ran for mayor, I knew I was running against people who were used to giving money to Coleman Young. I knew that, but I knew, also, that it was time for me to move on. I knew that if I lost, that it would be time to retire from public life. So I ran with the goal of inspiring women to consider running for higher office, and let God handle the outcome. I had enjoyed running for, and serving those 17 years that I sat on Detroit's City Council. Though I was humbled in the primary election, my candidacy kept the wheel of women being elected to higher offices, rolling. Today, we have thirty-four women representatives in the Michigan State legislature, 74 women in the United States Congress, including Michigan Senator Debbie Stabenow, and a woman, Jennifer Granholm, as the Governor of the State of Michigan. So a woman mayor isn't that far away.

Speaking of Senator Stabenow, it was Marianne Williamson, nationally and internationally known author and spiritual leader, who suggested to me that we get in touch with other spiritual women to pray for Debbie's election run in 2000. She was running against incumbent Spence Abraham, and was polling behind him months before the election. But many spiritual women gathered in my apartment every Saturday for about two months, leading up to the election. Debbie took over the lead in the polls, and defeated Abraham for the office. Another of the many miracles that occurred in my life so far.

Today, City Councilwoman Joann Watson is the only candidate that I've publicly endorsed for Detroit City Council, since my departure from the Council. I have known Joann for a number of years. She was with the YWCA, and became involved in the Women's Conference of Concerns. She was involved in helping battered women, is a former president of the Detroit chapter of the NAACP, and eventually became a radio personality, hosting her "Wake Up, Detroit" show on WHPR – FM. Both she and Ortheia Barnes-Kennerly are examples of women who have picked up where I have left off, both politically and spiritually.

Photos by Michael Kitchen

REV. ORTHEIA BARNES-KENNERLY & COUNCILWOMAN JOANN
WATSON
AT MY 84th BIRTHDAY PARTY

*****

Orlo Sauer stood by me during my years on Council, guiding me with my health. He still owned the store on Woodward and Six Mile Road, but the neighborhood was becoming over run with drug dealers. I knew that he would need to move. His wife was so afraid of the area, that she opened a store in Ferndale. They had the two health stores going at the same time. Then, one day, he tripped and fell out of a truck, landing on his hands, which ruined his career.

Shortly thereafter, while I was campaigning for mayor, Orlo took ill. I went to see him at Beaumont Hospital before I went to a Women's Conference of Concerns meeting. I parked the car and went into the hospital with a heavy heart, knowing that I was going to face the worst, but I didn't know what the worst was. When I arrived at his room, I was saddened by what I saw. The tall, handsome, strong man that was Orlo Sauer, was reduced to a dwarf, laying in the bed. He looked at me and said he was so glad to see me. "I knew you would come." I asked him where his wife was, and he said "she can't take this."

I sat and talked with him for a long time. I said, "Orlo, you can't go away because you have to write the book." He said, "I know. I got the papers back home." He always talked about how he was going to write a book about health. I said "Whose going to guide me through the rest of my life if I don't have your advice and help? You've got to fight back." He said, "I can't fight back any more." I scolded him. "Don't say that!"

Then, a number of doctors entered the room. They were hurried because of the data the machines hooked up to Orlo was telling them. They asked me to leave. As I was leaving, I heard him say, "Erma." I turned and looked at him as he raised his hands. "You write the book."

I cried all the way to the YWCA. Chuck Folks allowed us to hold the Women's Conference of Concerns meetings there. As I arrived, I received a phone call that Dorothy Knight had also died. I was trying to get to her after Orlo, for I hadn't seen her since she had gone into the hospital.

She had been with me from back in the 1943 riots, and was still with me through the years, even through council. Dorothy Knight was one of the first labor leaders that I helped. She was in a labor union in Hamtramck, an automobile union in the mid to late 1940's. I helped her run for secretary in the labor union, and she was the first African American and first woman to be a secretary in that union. She would climb ladders to nail my campaign posters up, when I ran for office. We worked together for many years in the community. My big regret is that I didn't get to see her before she passed.

When I lost Dorothy Knight, I lost a part of me. To lose her and Orlo Sauer in one night was a double blow that made me feel like I didn't want to stand up. I went on to the Women's Conference of Concerns meeting, and just briefly mentioned that I had lost two friends that night. It was such a devastating blow that it weakened my determination to stay on the council. It helped me determine that I was doing the right thing to come out, because I loved my friends. We weren't' getting any younger, and it was time to become even closer and more involved with them.

I had lost so many of my friends. Strong women like Gladys Woodward and 82 year-old, Camilla Lear, who were out there battling every day, to help me win. I don't even want to try naming them all, but they were symbolic of the beautiful church women who were helping me all the time.

So with the death of those two friends in that one night, my focus began to change, and I was glad that I was going to retire. I stayed close with Mrs. Sauer, and leant her the help of my office, to bury Orlo and to help her grieve the great loss. She could not take his death. She asked me to speak at his funeral, which was an honor for me. Here, when I first met them, they were a German couple who really didn't care to know any African Americans, or about African Americans, and yet, a relationship was developed between us that became so strong and lasting. I helped her handle the store, and tried to do some things for her. A staff member stepped up and was willing to help work with her.

She eventually developed cancer. Her niece from northern Michigan, came down to look after her, and trusted me enough to allow me the opportunity to help with Mrs. Sauer. The niece found out how much Mrs. Sauer loved me, that the Sauer family finally decided that someone had to continue the work of the Sauers' store.

When Mrs. Sauer died, her son and daughter, from the west, and her niece, asked me to conduct the service. I did, because I was honored to do so, and I had no right to ever refuse anyone who wanted my services as an ordained minister. And I needed no urging to do that, because my hand was in God's hand for whatever service I could give.

So there I was, the only African American in the whole funeral, conducting the funeral services for these German leaders, who were really fearful of African Americans, but who had loved me and trusted me, and worked with me through Equal Justice Council. I felt very fortunate to have known them. They taught me about German ancestry in America, about their family in Wisconsin that owned a farm where Orlo bought his goods, like wheat and honey. They taught me a lot about food, about what was in the food and what I should look for. And I kept in mind always Orlo's last words on this planet, "you write the book."

I've never written the book, but I've carried the book in my mind and heart. I don't dare speak about health, but I did mention my diet earlier, and maybe I'll be able to share more in another book.

The money that the Sours' children sold the store to me for, I never really was able to repay. The floor of the store was deteriorating. I couldn't risk having a health store in that location. So I moved to a location on Livernois. That building wasn't adequate for the amount of equipment and refrigeration that I had out in Ferndale. But it was the best I could do because that was all that was available and all I could afford. So I moved the store there. I had only one place to park, and every time I parked there, I had something stolen out of my car. It was a drug-addicted area that I had moved into. Even before I was on City Council, I tried to tell people that this drug society was coming and that we needed to act. But it was just overwhelming how it had swept throughout the community and the nation, over the years. It broke up families, and children were being contaminated because of drug houses across the street from the schools. It affected men and women, older and younger. It got to be too dangerous. The neighborhood was unsafe, and I lost customers because there was no place they could safely park.

I had gone on vacation for a week, and thought I left the store in the hands of someone I could trust. But he signed my name on checks to get what he wanted from the creditors, and made sales that did not go through the register, but into his pocket. I found out that I had been robbed by this person, and that caused me to close the store. Had it not been for a man I had met who owned a warehouse on the waterfront, I would not have had any help in moving the contents of my closed store. He was really just a delightful, earnest, sincere young man, and he brought in his crew and moved the stuff into his warehouse.

That was my focus after council. I wanted to go into the health business, to help all people, physically. But the years had taken its toll on me. I tried to make it work, as I would run from one health conference to another, trying to get a new business going, trying to get new products to help save families. I had left City Council, but had not left a rigorous life style. This ended up costing me my eyesight.

One day I was to put on a demonstration at a health conference. It went well. The next day, I was going to return to the conference, however, as I reached down to pick up my papers, I could no longer see. Had it not been for Jackie Woodson, who was there with me that day, I probably would not have been able to survive this blow that hit me. She put me in a car and drove me to the doctor's.

Jackie had been an assistant of mine at the health food store. As I was devastated by this sudden event, she assured me that she would not leave me as long as I needed her. She stayed with me and helped me for three years, taking care of me, and is still a close friend today.

*****

The first incident that informed me that my eyesight was a concern was during the time I was running for mayor. I was in Cleveland at the time, being honored at a national convention for an organization. When I was leaving the convention hall, I got into a cab. Suddenly, I had these flashes of light and color before me for a few seconds. When I returned to Detroit, I went to a doctor and explained to him what happened. He determined that I had cataracts, and though I was running for mayor, I could wait until after the campaign to have an operation.

Well, I've undergone five operations, three of them for cataracts, in an attempt to recover my eyesight. I think it hurt the doctor as much as it hurt me, that he did not succeed.

Since then, I have been committed to rebuilding and reestablishing my body as a whole temple, so that my eyesight would return. There are so many people who have helped me along the way, but I must mention Edith Brewster, who, for the last eight years or so, has been my prayer partner. Every morning we pray together, or if we cannot pray together in the morning, she'll read to me and pray with me in the evening.

But there was another lesson God had to teach me, and that was that I didn't need eyes to succeed. That I could do anything anyone else could do. I could talk, I could walk, I could climb stairs, I could travel across the country, I could lecture, I could sing, I could dance.

Photograph by Michael Kitchen

SPEAKING AT AN AWARD CEREMONY - 2001

And, I can share my life story with you, so that you can know that, anything in life is possible. You see, a little child from extremely humble beginning grew up as an African American woman, during a time in our nation when there was discrimination against both African Americans and women. Yet she climbed to great heights and overcame significant obstacles, and hopefully made the world a better place.

My message and blessing to you is:

YOU CAN, TOO!

EPILOGUE
Grand Rapids, Michigan - 1999

In the spring of 1999, the Michigan Women's Foundation awarded its inaugural Trillium Award for Lifetime Achievement. For the nine previous years, the organization held fundraising dinners and acknowledged the courage and achievements of individual Michigan women. However, this, their tenth year of honoring Michigan women, they created the Trillium Award to acknowledge the lifetime achievements of a Michigan woman. And I was the honored recipient.

This is truly an honor. My walls are filled with awards from all sorts of organizations, and some remain in storage because they have accumulated down through the years. I feel so honored and privileged that this little girl from Black Bottom could grow up to be a positive influence in the community. I am humbled to learn that I was able to touch the hearts of so many people in so many organizations that they felt so moved to present me with an award.

But this award was not only an honor to receive, but where it took me to receive it.

Two award dinners were to be held for the presentation of the award. One on the southeast side of Michigan, in Dearborn to be precise, just outside the city of Detroit. The other was to be held in Grand Rapids, the largest city on the southwest side of the state. More precisely, it was to be held in the Amway Grand Plaza Hotel - formerly known as the Pantland Hotel.

My former staff person, Betty Appleby, drove me out to Grand Rapids for the dinner celebration. My blindness prevented me from seeing the hotel, but I remembered the Pantland Hotel, and the reception I received when Geneva, Lela, Onslow and I arrived in 1938. The atmosphere was much different this time. I was treated with such kindness. The room that we stayed in was certainly more luxurious than the one the four of us crowded into six decades ago.

Each of the five award recipients were to speak before the organization after dinner. The other women were Alecia Woodrick, a philanthropist and activist; Pamela Aguirre, the CEO of Mexican Industries and benefactor to the Hispanic Community; Margaret Taylor Smith, the first woman Board Chairman of the Kresge Foundation; and Elizabeth Upjohn Mason, a committed volunteer and foundation leader. I was the only one to be receiving the Lifetime Achievement award.

It eventually came my turn to speak. I started with a little joke about the Trillium Award, saying how I thought it had something to do with the coming millennium, until someone had told me that the Trillium was a flower.

Then, standing there in the hotel where I had to stand firm to get the room we reserved over sixty years ago, I shared the story with the audience. About the clerk's insistence that there was no room for my friends and myself. About the maitre de taking us to the lavish home away from the hotel, in hopes of hosting us in a location that was not the hotel. And most importantly, about our singing protest, in the lobby and throughout the convention hall that we had to register in. "God Bless America." the hymn of our protest.

As I ended my speech with gratitude for being the recipient of such an award, I could feel the intensity of the applause as the dinner guests acknowledged me. But then, someone from the back began singing. A single voice, that became two, then more, then finally into a crescendo of song that reached deep into my heart.

"God Bless America," they sang. God Bless America.

*****

You will find that when you get involved in something, like a cause that you know is right, or a movement that you know in your heart is in line with your purpose, and that the benefactors are others and not yourself, you've been brought to it by the power and Spirit of God, however you may define God. You will also be faced with obstacles. Some obstacles may be minor hurdles that need to be leapt over to get to your desired outcome. Some obstacles may look like mountains before you, that may take a lifetime of commitment to get over. Know that if it is in your heart to pursue it, the struggle will be worth it for those you are seeking to help, and yourself.

In 1938, I faced discrimination that was the status quo of that day. In 1999, the status quo had changed. God had a role for me to play in that change. God has a role for you, in some way. You don't necessarily need to go looking for it. God will bring it to you. And your heart will tell you to pursue it. Pursue it with love and light, and do not fear the obstacles. Before you know it, your whole world will change on you, and it will be for the better.

APPENDIX A

<u>Erma Henderson's Inaugural Messages</u>
<u>As President of the Detroit City Council</u>

Detroit City Council President

Erma Henderson's Message

Delivered January 4, 1978

People involvement and cooperation became the crucial key to the work of our city's most successful council efforts over the past four years. People involvement is still the key to our continuing growth, development, prosperity and peace of our community.

As public servants, being inaugurated today, we pledge that we will work together to realize the hopes and dreams which we share to make Detroit the most enlightened city of our times.

We were once known as the motor capital of the world - a city that through unity and cooperation, mounted the world on wheels.

The future beckons to us to accept the challenges of leadership in our nation and in our world. This time, we shall not only be known for singular industries, but for our ability to become the heart of the greatest megalopolis on the globe. This will raise our people to new heights of dignity and progress. As president, I will seek a blending of our spiritual qualities that we may rise out of the devastating ashes of the past to stabilize our neighborhoods - rehabilitating and conserving that which we cherish - then moving on to build new homes, new parks, new systems of health care, new modes of transportation, new commercial and industrial development.

As our mayor continues to accept the vital challenges of this day, we - as members of the City Council - will work with him in good will and understanding of our common directions.

We accept the mandate of the voters of this city who spoke loudly in support of a job and training program for our youth and chronically unemployed; who cried out against the blight and decay of our neighborhood - whether caused by the callous action of industry - or a combination of industry and government - who redlined us so sufficiently that our homes, our neighborhoods, our security has been almost irreparably damaged beyond traditional means of repair.

Yes, you demand an end to crime, and together we are working to protect our neighborhoods by building block after block of citizen concern and citizen goodwill.

You, the people, rejected encroachment of blight through lack of environmental protection, and we are a cleaner, healthier city who accepts the further challenge to end all forms of contamination.

You, the people, agree with us that our city government must act in concert with all other forms of government to provide the best education possible, to establish full equality of opportunity; and to enhance the quality of life for our senior citizens who continue to lay foundations of truth and dignity for tomorrow.

We accept your mandate. No one of us, however, as members of our council, can be successful in our efforts unless you, the people of the city, are once again completely involved. We are not afraid to dig deeply - or aim high. But, we need your strength, your full capacity to care, your harmonious coordination of effort, your determination, to help us achieve our mutual goals.

We pray that God will bless you, and yours, throughout these challenging four years to come. It will be an exciting and enjoyable experience if we continue to work together.

Detroit City Council President

Erma Henderson's Message

Ford Auditorium

January 5, 1982

We have gathered here tonight to proclaim once again that, despite our hardships, we shall not be moved.

We shall not be moved from our determination to save our city. We are unique in American life for, while the federal government has determinedly stripped us from the kind of support we desperately need for our aged, our poor, our children, and our handicapped, we are steadily breaking ground to build a newer and greater Detroit.

Eleven representatives of the people have been elected to serve this four-year term. If we serve our charter-mandated functions, then we serve well. If we act upon the courage of our convictions we serve better! That means that we may not always agree, but we can wrestle with the problems out in the open for all to hear, see and know what super-human efforts we are pledged to make, in cooperation with our mayor and each other, in order to rescue those who are hungry, naked, and outdoors, mentally, physically and spiritually.

Council, to me, is like the story of the little Dutch boy who stood with his finger in the dyke holding back the mighty rushing waters. We stand today as bulwarks against the ever encroaching danger that comes from the highest rate of unemployment since the great depression. That danger is a denial to the God-given right to use our minds to improve our lot by closing the door to education for the masses; that danger is a denial to those who are handicapped; that danger is a denial to those who have lived their lives in the hope that their own contributions to social security would be sufficient to provide them with dignity and courage as seniors. Shall we lay down, roll over and play dead? That is the challenge. We say no!

I understand that there are some billboards around town which read, "Stay Tough Detroit - Things Will Get Better," and that's our sentiment exactly.

The automobile industry revolutionized the world and put Detroit on the map. Now, some people say that America's love affair with the automobile is over. We, in Detroit, do not believe that, and we intend to use every effort and every available means to revitalize our industries so that Detroit will not become a ghost town.

Our mayor has given great and determined leadership in this city, and he has been aided and supported by the necessary council votes for every program on the drawing board, and we are proud of that. The next four years will find us ready, willing, and able to sacrifice whatever it takes for our offices to work in behalf of the people. I repeat, people...for people in our neighborhoods; people in our homes, our churches and our schools. For people are the force we will use to hold back the tide of ignorance and despair.

We are a multi-ethnic, multi-racial community. While we are not naive enough to think Detroit is a melting pot, we are determined that we will close the cultural gaps that separate us as we move forward together to face a new beginning. We will not move ahead in this computer electronic technological age selfishly. We will develop trade with the under-developed countries and exchange skills as one means of solving our employment problems. We look forward to the stimulation of this trade by making our Detroit River the most viable inland water port in the world.

While federal government is attempting to preempt the field of communications, Detroit will proceed to regulate and develop new technological industries such as bringing cable television to Detroit.

In the meantime, we will exercise our legislative functions and continue to be an effective liaison between the citizens of Detroit and the executive branch.

Detroit City Council President

Erma Henderson's Message

January 10, 1986

Ford Auditorium

First, allow me to thank God, and thank you, the citizens of Detroit for re-electing this entire City Council, thus giving us the opportunity to work for you four more years.

Your faith and trust has given us the honor of being the first full council to be re-elected in its entirety in two decades. For this, we will earnestly try, each in our own way, to give you, our very best committed service.

So that the historic significance of these proceedings is properly documented for future generations, let it be recorded that you have elected the first mayor in the City's history to serve an unprecedented 4th term and the first Council President in the City's history to serve an unprecedented 3rd term.

You say by your actions that you have faith to believe that this Council, this Mayor, and this City Clerk will meet the challenge of these days of crises and change.

The economic times of our day portrays the contradictions of our society. The December 26th cover story of USA Today, for example, reported a prediction that falling interest rates, a weakening dollar, and a surging bull market will spur the economy to grow a strong 5.2% in 1986. On the other hand, a further prediction was made that a sharp slow down in consumer business, and government spending, would drag the economy into a mild recession. The most urgent analysis for Detroit, however, is that the unemployment rate will remain steady, despite the fact that costs of food, clothing, shelter, and health care will steadily rise.

At a recent National League of Cities Annual Convention, I was shocked to see the number of elected officials from small cities around the Country who supported the Reagan Administration's negative policy for cities. This is a clear signal that we may very well lose revenue sharing which now takes care of our public safety and sanitation needs. It also drives home the point that there is no guarantee that Community Development Block Grants will continue. Our neighborhood improvement projects will suffer a great loss if we lose these programs on a national basis. And this will be in addition to the continued dismantling of essential services through the agencies that deal with Health, Education and Social Welfare.

In an effort to cushion the negatives of this current national threat to the survival of urban cities, we pledge our full faith efforts to leave no stone unturned to guarantee that despite whatever befalls us from the federal cutbacks, we will proceed with renewed strength and determination to give our fullest measure to the people of Detroit. Let's take a close look at our Detroit. On the one hand, Detroit has the highest rate of unemployment of Black youth in this country, while on the other hand, there is a steady rising of our middle class young Black people who have captured a positive glimpse of the future, and are steadily moving upwards on the economic ladder. On the one hand, Detroit is a major victim of the abominable drug traffic, while on the other hand, we are a model city in cutting our crime rate and leading whole communities in the struggle. Detroit is seeing more and more of its city become a visual wasteland accelerated by one national policy that led to the skeletons we see in housing today. Skeletons that have to be demolished or rehabilitated for the sake of our safety and sanity. Detroit's ailing transportation system - like other urban cities, will probably never again be supported by the fare-box alone.

According to most dismal predictions, Detroit should be down on its knees about now, but not all of us agree with those who perpetuate an on-again, off-again, love/hate relationship with our city.

We must measure Detroit's greatness by its people. We must not expect that things will be done today as they were done 40 years ago when our city's transportation system was not tax supported, and when the city owned a city university and the public school system. Our present time must not be compared to abnormal times when throngs came to Detroit for defense jobs which were expected to decrease at war's end.

Those of us who measure our greatness by peace time, rather than war time, must certainly have a clear vision of what we are capable of becoming.

Detroit is rapidly making its transition into high technology and is working towards becoming a major force in the international trade market. Detroit is also enjoying the prominence of a world renowned Cultural Center, and is the home of the finest Medical Center in America.

Detroit is the Home of Champions who know what it is to gird our collective lives for battle. We know how to rally together for our survival. We have built sky-scrapers out of despair, and we are determined that whatever negative economic predictions, whatever negative federal policies are developed, Detroit will stand tall like a might army led by those eleven you have elected.

You have established, through mandate, a system of checks and balances, and we are sworn to protect that sacred trust, though we may not always agree with the Executive Branch. Our differences are never personal, or big enough, to stop our united goal, for we are equally proud that together we have made a lasting contribution to the revitalization of Detroit. Our record speaks for itself, for we have approved every major development in this City.

As your public servants, we gently ask you to command us wisely and to preserve the spirit of unity and cooperation which this occasion is meant to express. We pledge our continued support to our dynamic Mayor as we move forward together, propelling Detroit into a blueprint for change that will be an inspiration for generations to come.

Let each of us go down from this place today with renewed determination and vigor to keep the peace, to restore harmony, and to encourage love and concern for all of our people in this, the greatest city in America, the City of Champions, the City of Detroit.

APPENDIX B

ELECTION RESULTS

1969

1.	Mel Ravitz	316,062
2.	Nicholas Hood	267,006
3.	Carl Levin	250,122
4.	David Eberhard	235,174
5.	Robert Tindal	221,152
6.	William G. Rogell	215,662
7.	Philip Van Antwerp	211,257
8.	Anthony Wierzbicki	206,326
9.	Ernest Browne Jr.	192,890
10.	Blanche Parent White	190,299
11.	Jack Kelley	187,105
12.	Norbert Wierszewski	159,172
13.	Richard Carey	153,060
14.	James Frazer	142,904
15.	Erma Henderson	138,641

1973

1.	Erma Henderson	170,598
2.	Jack Kelley	163,189

1974

1.	Carl Levin	280,253
2.	Nicholas Hood	262,794
3.	Erma Henderson	241,547
4.	Ernest C. Browne Jr.	230,530
5.	Clyde Cleveland	177,150
6.	Maryann Mahaffey	173,742
7.	William G. Rogell	170,410
8.	David Eberhard	159,801
9.	Jack Kelley	157,144

1977

1.	Erma Henderson	244,395
2.	Maryann Mahaffey	231,487
3.	Nicholas Hood	231,480
4.	Clyde Cleveland	187,029
5.	Jack Kelley	183,591
6.	David Eberhard	170,744
7.	Ken Cockrel	166,593
8.	William G. Rogell	147,348
9.	Herbert McFadden Jr.	119,736

1981

1.	Erma Henderson	194,235
2.	Nicholas Hood	172,448
3.	Maryann Mahaffey	163,781
4.	Clyde Cleveland	154,161
5.	Jack Kelley	139,199
6.	Mel Ravitz	135,106
7.	Barbara Rose Collins	129,565
8.	David Eberhard	104,293
9.	John Peoples	97,668

1985

1.	Erma Henderson	90,509
2.	Nicholas Hood	82,523

3.	Maryann Mahaffey	76,564
4.	Clyde Cleveland	73,711
5.	Mel Ravitz	67,580
6.	Jack Kelley	62,506
7.	Barbara Rose Collins	59,798
8.	David Eberhard	57,002
9.	John Peoples	48,110

SOURCES

Books

Detroit Free Press, edited by Peter Gavrilovich and Bill McGraw, The Detroit Almanac: 300 Years of Life in the Motor City, Detroit Free Press, 2000.

City of Detroit, Journal of the City Council - For the years 1968 - 1989.

King Jr., Martin Luther, edited by Clayborne Carson, The Autobiography of Martin Luther King Jr., New York, Warner Books, 1998.

Wilson, Sunnie with John Cohassey, Toast of the Town: The Life and Times of Sunnie Wilson, Wayne State University Press, 1998.

Young, Coleman, with Lonnie Wheeler, Hard Stuff: The Autobiography of Mayor Coleman Young, New York, Viking, 1994.

Articles

"African Chamber of Commerce meets in Detroit" American Musulm Journal, September 3, 1982

"African Trade Conference July 28-31 at Cobo Hall," Michigan Chronicle, July 10, 1982.

"Cobo Hall Trade Conference. Invest in Africa, Michigan Firms are Told." Detroit Free Press, July 29, 1982.

"Common Council Candidate is Community Interest Custodian," Michigan Chronicle, November 1, 1969.

"Council Candidate Plans To Avoid Racial Overtone." Detroit News, April 17, 1972.

"Council Members Say Detroit Could Learn From Soviet City." Detroit Free Press, January 7, 1985.

"Councilwoman Takes Seat; Council Full." Detroit Free Press, November 28, 1972

"Detroit Delegation in Montenegro. Objective - Cooperation." Pobjeda, (Montenegro, Yugoslavia), June 26, 1988 (translated by Margaret Fishman).

"Detroit's New Councilman a Quiet Fighter," Detroit News, November 9, 1972.

"Detroiters Praise Grenada, Council Condemns Invasion" Detroit Free Press, October 27, 1983.

"Detroiters Vow To Fight High Insurance Costs." Michigan Chronicle, September 24, 1988.

"Forum Examines State of World's Women," Detroit Free Press, July 10, 1985.

"Henderson Charges Lag On Redlining" Detroit News, August 19, 1981.

"Ideas to Span the Spheres. Michigan And Africa Try Trading Goods, Culture and Education." Detroit Free Press, December 15, 1982.

"If You Think You Came From Nowhere, Then There's No Place You Can Go." Insight, October 1970.

"Insurance Companies Next. Red Line Still Drawn" Lansing Star, Week Ending October 11, 1978.

"Last Week, the Detroit City Council President, Erma Henderson, Was Hosted by Titograd and Montenegro." Titograd Tribune (Yugoslavia), July 1, 1988 (translated by Margaret Fishman)

"Mrs. Henderson tops Kelley in Council Race" Detroit News, November 10, 1972.

"Robeson Remebered." Detroit Free Press, April 17, 1990.

"UN Ready to Aid in Crisis, Women's Conference Told," Detroit Free Press, May 2, 1982

"The Very Image of Grace," Detroit Free Press, June 17, 2001.

"Women aid Mrs. Henderson," Detroit News, August 5, 1973.

"Women's Vote Emphasized by Mrs. Henderson." Detroit News, November 2, 1973.

"Yesterday in Belgrade Detroit Delegation Leaves Country." Pobjeda (Montengro, Yugoslavia), July 5, 1988 (translated by Margaret Fishman)

Websites

"The Benevolent & Protective Order of Elks of the USA," www.elks. org/enf/fastfacts.cfm.

"Biography: Paul Robeson" http://homepage.sunrise.ch/homepage/ comtex/rob3.htm

"The Character of Anti-Semitism in America, 1940-1976" http://www. umich.edu/~bhl/bhl/topics/antisem.htm.

"Detroit African-American History Project" www.daahp.wayne.edu.

"Erma Henderson: For the People adn Of the People" Michigan Chronicle, October 28, 1972.

"The Essential Insurance Act" www.insure.com/states/mi/eia/html.

"Gerald Smith" http://www.spartacus.schoolnet.co.uk/USAsmithGLK. htm.

"Henry A. Wallace" www.geocities.com/redencyclopedia/bios/wallace.htm

"The Improved Benevolent Protective Order of Elks of the World" www.northbysouth.org/2000/Fraternal/ibpoew.htm

"The Invasion of Grenada" www.historyguy.com/Grenada.html.

"The Little Rock Nine: Integrating Central High" http://littlerock.about.com/library/weekly/aa020200a.htm.

"Michigan Women's Foundation Trillium." www.lib.msu.edu/harris23/grants/tril99su.htm

"The Murder of Emmett Till" www.stanford.edu/~tommyz/1950's/Emmit%20Till.htm

"Paul Robeson" www.rutgers.edu/robeson.html

"United Nation's Conference on Women," http://atdpweb.soe.berkeley.edu/quest/herstory/Beijing.html

"Universal Negro Improvement Association and African Communities League" www.unia-acl.org.

"Women in Municipal Government" www.nlc.org/nlc_org/site/membership/constituency_groups/wimg.cfm

Other

Erma Henderson Campaign "73" Issues booklet.

Erma Henderson For Mayor Track Record booklet

Erma Henderson's Wholistic Health Food Store Grand Opening program

Written and Oral Interviews with:
- Betty Appleby
- Reverend Ortheia Barnes-Kennerly
- Laura Lee Bowman
- Edith Brewster

222

- Dr. Arthur Carter
- Councilman Clyde Cleveland
- Dr. Bernadine Denning
- Michael Descamps
- Al Fishman
- Margaret Fishman
- Bessie Watters Gabriel
- Esther Hopkins
- Irma Jaxson
- Dr. Leno Art Jaxson
- Millie Jeffrey
- Mary Frances Lewis
- Councilwoman Maryann Mahaffey
- Nellie Moore
- Earlene Morris
- Ruth Mosley
- Dr. Mary Frances Myler
- Louis Pettiway
- Pauline Reese
- Coco Shindi
- Marilyn Shorr
- Dr. Mary Speed
- Councilwoman Alberta Tinsley-Talabi
- Jackie Woodson

MCL Sec. 500.1501 et seq.

Progress Report and Major Findings of the Equal Justice Council Court Watcher Study in Detroit Recorder's Court - Donald I. Warren, The University of Michigan.

About the Author

Erma Henderson served on the Detroit City Council from 1973 through 1989. Filling the vacant seat left open by the death of Robert Tindal, she became the first African American woman to serve on Detroit's City Council, with her victory in the run-off election of 1972. She won her seat again in the 1973 election, then followed with overwhelming victories in 1977, 1981, and 1985, making her the first African American to be elected Detroit City Council President, and the only person to have held that position for three consecutive terms.

Born in 1917, her life has been committed to social activism, racial and cultural inclusion, democratic ideals and spiritual principles. She has spoken nationally and internationally on these topics.

Printed in the United States
20504LVS00001B/343

9 781418 422912